# SCIENTOLOGY

## THE NOW RELIGION

# SCIENTOLOGY

## THE NOW RELIGION

*by George Malko*

DELACORTE PRESS / NEW YORK

I would like to thank Michaela Williams, articles editor
of the now defunct *eye* Magazine,
who invited me to write an article
about Scientology. Research into the subject
led to this book, which contains most
of the material from that original
article, but in much different form.
*G.M.*

Grateful acknowledgment is made for permission to quote
from the following copyrighted material:

*Nine Chains to the Moon* by Buckminster Fuller:
Used by permission of Southern Illinois University Press.

Extracts from *Scientologie 34* by A. Nordenholz,
translated by W. R. McPheeters:
Used by permission of W. R. McPheeters,
P. O. Box 641, Lucerne Valley, California 92356.

"The Polygraph" by Burke M. Smith:
Copyright © 1967 by Scientific American, Inc.
All rights reserved. Used by permission.

*To the memory of*
*my father*

"... miracles don't happen.
It's always the apparatus
and the spiel which have to
do the work. The clergy
have the same sad experience.
God is silent and people chatter."

INGMAR BERGMAN
in *The Magician*

# INTRODUCTION

On Sunday, December 22, 1968, John McMaster, the world's first *clear*—a being enlightened and totally free—spoke at the weekly services of New York's Church of Scientology. The church is headquartered at 49 West 32nd Street in the main ballroom of the Hotel Martinique, a moderately priced establishment of well-worn respectability which is just off Herald Square, on the fringes of the bustling crowds that daily attack Macy's, Gimbel's, and E.J. Korvette. I had been in the ballroom once before, at a Scientology congress. Then, the large high-ceilinged room had been a dun-yellow, with something used and shabby about it. Now, presumably in honor of McMaster's singular appearance, the whole room had been painted white and the ceiling had been cleaned. Because it was approaching Christmas, there were decorations and a tinseled tree.

The proceedings began with some singing of blues songs by a girl named Doreen Davis. She introduced each song with a few simple appropriate words, linking them to Scientology if possible, to what she had learned from being part of it. She was well received and then introduced her accompanist, Amanda Ambrose, herself an accomplished blues singer, who followed Miss Davis and sang a few more songs, finishing with what was obviously the gathering's favorite, "On A Clear Day You Can See Forever."

The room was packed. There must have been four hundred

people there, filling all the seats and crowding the narrow aisles. In the back, in areas usually partitioned off into small offices, the partitions had been pushed back and people stood on desks, a few having scrambled up to sit on filing cabinets. A little boy, not at all lost, pushed his way with young determination among the people crowding everywhere, the sweat shirt he wore bearing the announcement "Scientology Works!" At the front of the room, dominating everything, was an enormous black and white photograph of L. Ron Hubbard, the man who had devised and developed all of the basic theories and teaching techniques of Scientology, from its melodramatic beginnings as Dianetics to the present day and its promise of the realization of one's *theta,* one's true spirit. It was an imposing photograph, a head shot, three-quarters face, his chin resting on the thumbs of his joined hands, his receding white hair smoothly combed back from a high forehead, his eyes slightly narrowed giving him something of a vulpine look. It was a study in self-confidence.

Then McMaster was announced and appeared. He was wearing clerical garb and a clerical collar, white cuffs of a thin wool turtleneck showing at the wrists of his black jacket. He had a purple sash around his neck, with some kind of pendant hanging just at the juncture of the jacket, under the button. McMaster, a one-time medical student who was born in South Africa, is of indeterminate age, anywhere from forty-two to fifty. His features are very fine and his face is soft, almost beautiful, almost ascetic, with very clear light blue eyes that always gaze out peacefully, with only one or two moments when, while making a point, they widen the way William F. Buckley's do when he is on to something pertinent and rich on the tongue to say. McMaster's hair is corn-silk blond and looks whitened by the sun. His hands, as he speaks, move slightly, airily, meeting in front to let fingers touch in the barest kind of clasp.

He began almost immediately by telling of his experiences

with a television program, the Alan Burke Show, which had invited him to appear to talk about Scientology. He had arrived at the studio, he said, and found that people he knew to be hostile to Scientology had been placed in the studio audience to question him when open questioning was invited. Challenging the program's producer on this, McMaster said the man had explained the program was merely trying to present both sides of the subject. McMaster, looking out at us with the same calm he had shown the producer, told the man, "How can there be two sides to the truth?" and walked out.

The audience loved it! They applauded warmly, very very warmly, and watched him as he spoke with a kind of adoring, sure hunger, knowing that here was the proof, the living proof, that everything they were studying and absorbing and accepting and agreeing upon led *somewhere*. McMaster said "reality is *agreement*," and spoke of the warmth he felt emanating from the gathering, and how the last time he had spoken in New York there was so much agreement it was as if the entire Hotel Martinique would rise and float gently down Broadway. The audience laughed again and clapped, knowing it wouldn't be so, knowing they could do it if they wanted to, but it didn't have to be challenged. Because they believed it, and John McMaster believed it, and their *agreement* was all that counted. "Scientology," he said, "is essentially the study of truth. . . ." "The basic human right," he said, "is the right to be you."

There were many children in the hall. Their parents let them wander with a kind of soft indulgence, and the children were never in the way; one little girl wandered from person to person, reaching up to grasp a lapel clumsily and be helped up onto a lap, there to sit and listen for a while until the urge to move on made her slide back down to the floor and continue her wanderings. Another tot, barely walking, clutched a man's knee, tears coursing down her little face. The man, who was not her father, soothed her with gentle words and picked her up and held her in his lap. In two minutes the child was asleep. In front of me, a mother wearing bell-bottomed denims, her light chestnut hair "natural," round-rimmed granny glasses on her nose, raised her poor-boy knit T-shirt and suckled her tiny son, who had been whimpering uncomfortably. Nobody seemed to mind. Here was fellowship, communion, understanding, *agreement*. And all the while McMaster, exuding something enormously benign, spoke on, about levels of agreement, about "Ron" being just somebody who was offering the world liberation, about the love he sensed around him, about— all of a sudden a digression, and he shifted his stance because he wanted us to know what had happened—wandering into one of the porny-type magazine and book stores next to the Hotel Dixie where he was staying and seeing the covetous quality of the guarded browsings of the men there, saddened to think it could not be all out in the open. It was, to me, a curious admission of appetite, and I admired McMaster for bringing it up: into the bookstore, masses of photo books, the young men pictured lax and bland-faced, pendants drooping, legs asunder, strength seeped out, eyes watching, waiting, some half-closed, a few smiles, so little joy.

McMaster continued speaking with an infinite calm which seemed to emanate from some deep wellspring of febrile tension kept in extraordinary check. He interspersed what he said with moments of light, graceful wit. He bathed us all in the loving clarity of Scientology's sweet reason. Then he was finished, and the congregation rose, applauding wildly, unable to make their hands and the expressions on their faces communicate what they really felt for him as he moved sideways to an exit, raising his arm in gentle benediction, stopping to accept an embrace from a girl, nothing shy, no embarrassment —were the Apostles embarrassed?—continuing to the door, turning once more, right hand raised, a blessing, a grateful farewell, and he was gone.

The hall emptied slowly but I lingered behind, and turning, I found myself once more staring at the photograph of L. Ron Hubbard, the man whose inventive genius had allowed Mc-Master to become the world's first *clear*. What he had said, I realized with some surprise, had not impressed me very much. In the now almost empty room, I barely remembered whether or not he had actually spoken on any particular theme. Only one thing stuck in my mind, and I saw him saying it once more, fingers of his hands touching to form a delicate bridge, his eyes slowly sweeping all of us with a look both generous and shy: "How can there be two sides to the truth?"

# ONE

ONE

# THE NOW RELIGION ||||

I was never indifferent, or uninformed. Scientology, I had once written, was a Reality of its own, using techniques which draw on various principles: "Confession" similar to that developed by Frank Nathan Daniel Buchman, father of the Moral Re-Armament movement; Émile Coué's self-improvement teachings ("Every day and in every way, I am becoming better and better"); with elements of sensitivity training and encounter-sessions, those now-popular seventy-two-hour group encounters where exhaustion finally leaves you with shredded nerve ends ready to absorb anything.

As a unique Reality, Scientology is, I realized, manifestly ready—and more than a little able—to absorb *people*. Scientology spokesmen now claim a worldwide church membership of 15,000,000. Figures for the United States vary, but it is said that Scientology enjoys a membership of 250,000 in California alone—double the number of a year ago. As for income, the estimated weekly gross in this country is $1.4 million. And I think that these membership and weekly gross figures are modest.

I had also heard various stories, had been told things, and had read things.

Scientology was dangerous. A housewife in Los Angeles put $4,000 into Scientology processing because she was told it would help her overcome her frigidity. It didn't work. Her husband divorced her.

3

Scientology is insidiously taking over. In England, a village where Scientology had set up its world headquarters was supposedly being "bought up" by the movement, house by house and business by business.

Scientology is a con game. According to the records of one police department in this country, a millionaire in Florida who said he suffered from acute "nervousness" turned to Scientology after both Johns Hopkins and the Mayo Clinic found nothing wrong with him. Twenty-eight thousand dollars and two years later, he was still convinced Scientology processing would help him.

Scientology is "an evil cloud," which "settles on a person." In Sydney, Australia, a judge sentenced a man to prison for the mishandling of funds, and said, "It is clear that a good deal of your mental difficulty is due to your association with people who call themselves Scientologists." He went on to label it "an evil cloud."

"You could make a very cruel statement," said one former Scientologist who had spent enough time close to its hot center to be convinced he knew what he was talking about, "and say that Scientology is a kind of spiritual fascism. My analogy is a little ruthless, and a more fair way of saying it is that there are elements of dictatorship in it as an organization, which is basically a spiritual organization derived from a spiritual understanding and methods of spiritual advancement."

But I also met scores of young people, some of them the youthful drifters now becoming such a wrenching sight in our cities, others high school and college dropouts, all of whom spoke with fervid sincerity and enthusiasm as they told me of incredible personal gains they had made in Scientology, how they had suddenly "seen themselves" for the first time. They were, particularly in the strange conformity of their dedication, very much like a subculture, similar to many of the serious and sincere members of acid and pot subcultures I've known, glowing with that special, private knowledge and fund of insights which is so much of the strength which brings and holds them together. Comparably, what Scientologists feel they possess is so extraordinary, so marvelous, that only giving it, forcing it if necessary, upon the rest of mankind, will fulfill the promise of this cherished treasure. They spoke of the beauty in themselves they had never known existed, how Scientology's teachings and techniques had opened doors they thought forever closed. "The whole world has come alive," wrote one. "I can't remember when I have felt so great!" wrote another. "The most important factor," wrote a third, "was that I gained *awareness*." The one very important contrast to our other modern subcultures was that all these kids seemed to be contradicting the popular notion of disillusioned youth as they energetically embraced a philosophy which not only welcomed them with open arms, but seemed to show them A Way which was foolproof.

So strong is Scientology in attracting these kids that in some instances it has done more than simply alienate children from their parents. I met one family where the total, absolute involvement of the children resulted in such a cataclysmic break, such a destruction of all the bonds which had kept six people together and sustained them as a family that, in desperation, the mother had decided to get into Scientology to try and understand what it was that had, in effect, taken her children from her. Within months—she told me all this in a voice which dropped at times to a nervous, confidential whisper, rising at other times to declare, posit, be strong and confident—within months she had become convinced that she had discovered a philosophy which did work, just as her children claimed, and she was certain it would eventually help her as much as it had helped them. She argued sincerely that she had experienced all of the soul-illuminating insights Scientology promises mankind. When I asked her what her husband thought of what she had done, she grew hesitant, almost confused, and finally confessed she couldn't begin to describe the bitterness he felt.

He had, I realized with a shock as she tried to explain the situation, been betrayed by his entire family and now he was the outsider who refused to open his eyes and "see" the truth. Not only did he no longer know what it was that had taken his sons and daughters from him, but now he watched his wife struggle to conform to this new philosophical religion, struggling to make herself believe that through passionate acceptance of all that Scientology promises, she would achieve the only thing which really had ever mattered to her, the rediscovery and salvation of her children.

Who was she, I wondered, really? Chain-smoking nervously, getting up repeatedly to refresh her drink, jumping in her conversation from one aspect of Scientology to another, making oblique references to one daughter who was off at one of Scientology's centers, to a son who was somewhere else, to her husband, whose reasonable efforts to make his own traditional, almost scholarly doubts known to all of them had been ignored and rejected with that merciless and arrogant confidence of the blind believer. . . . Who was she? What had happened to her, and her children? How had it been done? What was I investigating, a genuine religion, which Scientology quite legally claims to be, or something much simpler yet at the same time incredibly more insidious, some subtle union of *The Power of Positive Thinking*, a Dale Carnegie course, some kind of self-hypnosis, and a liberal spicing of a most refined science fiction?

It was a long time before I found out. My ambivalence was based, partly, on a reluctance to go out and find the flaws in what a lot of people looked at as being their religion. You just don't go out and knock a religion. Just the same, there was this freaky faddishness to the whole thing, everybody talking about the celebrities getting into it: Leonard Cohen, and Tennessee Williams—prior to his conversion—and William Burroughs, and then you hear that Cass Elliot got her Grades down in St.

Thomas. Movie Star Stephen Boyd, a Grade IV Release at the time, wrote an enthusiastic letter to Scientology describing how he had used his newfound abilities to survive the rigors of location shooting in Louisiana. And now the word is that the Beatles are definitely interested! And Jim Morrison! Official Scientology publications are emphasizing the big names. "That's the sign," it said in a recent issue of *The Auditor,* the monthly journal of Scientology. "Remember twenty years ago," it went on, "when artists were taking up psychoanalysis? It's always the beginning of the big win when celebrities—songwriters, actors, artists, writers, begin to take something up."

The big win. Or as Bob Thomas, a minister of the Church of Scientology who is now executive director of Scientology for the continental United States and probably the highest-ranking scientologist in the country, called it: "the most vital new movement in America today." Wherever you go, the Scientology word is being shouted at you from Dayglo posters showing an exultantly leaping man, his very vibrancy dividing his body into a discord of parallel striations. Pick up your telephone in New York and dial 565-3878, and you hear: "Hello. This is a recording inviting you to step into the exciting world of the totally free, the world of Scientology. Find out who you really are. Discover your real abilities, and how you can be in control of your own life once again. Attend our free film presentation at two P.M. every day and at four and seven-thirty Monday through Friday at forty-nine West Thirty-second Street. That's the corner of Broadway. Also, at the sound of the tone leave your name and address, and we will mail you a free information packet. And *thank you* for calling." If you leave your name and address you are bombarded by a direct-mail campaign which urges you to take courses! buy books! bring friends! On street corners everywhere attractive-looking young people hand out cards in the form of tickets which read: Admit One To Total Freedom—Film and Talk, What Scientology Is. Every evening of every day introductory sessions are being held in cities all over the world. The Big Win for the Big Now Religion.

Bob Thomas is a very large fleshy man with a high forehead and long, fine brown hair worn thickly combed back, giving him the appearance of a somewhat enormous George Washington. His New York office, where we spoke the first time I saw him, was tastefully decorated, with a handsome red wall-to-wall carpet, paintings on the wall, and well-chosen, comfortable furniture. His large desk had a white push-button telephone on one side and a Sony cassette tape recorder on the other. As we talked, he often leaned back to put his alligator loafers up on the desk. To the front of the desk, right in front of the leather armchair I was sitting in, was an E-Meter, Scientology's basic and all-important auditing tool, with his name Dymo-taped on it. Behind the desk, to the right as I faced him, books were lined up on top of a radiator which was under an air conditioner. Though the weather outside had turned brisk, the air conditioner was on. Thomas chain-smoked Spring menthol cigarettes during our talk, and over my right shoulder, on a dresser, a color television set was on, Walter Cronkite drumming Vietnam casualty figures into my ear. I looked at the books on the radiator and noticed Adam Smith's *The Money Game,* and next to it, on its side, a paperback copy of Norman O. Brown's *Love's Body.* Thomas was telling me why so many young people in particular are being drawn to Scientology.

"Scientology has the answers these kids are looking for, plus all the ingredients of novelty, freshness, and depth. It doesn't have the old pat answers, and it validates creativity." I asked if Scientology was replacing drugs for some of them. "The drug experience," he explained in a manner which was frank and direct, using Scientology's private lingo sparingly, "produces a kind of artificially induced insight into some of the more metaphysical aspects of man's consciousness. But it's very frustrating because it is limiting, and now here's Scientology, a drugless psychedelic—using the exact meaning of the word *psychedelic*, which is soul-expanding—which deals in the very same insights *without* drugs. We provide the philosophical background which can be understood by young people who have taken drugs and have seen the dead end of drugs, but who are still haunted by the visions they saw. Scientology is a root to the achievement of some of these awarenesses on a natural basis, by natural means. In a warped way, kids under drugs *have* seen themselves, but that is *at effect*, not *at cause*."

But what *is* it, I wondered. Did I really have to achieve an understanding of a new theology and disciplines similar to canon law? Wasn't there some simple statement which would make it all fall into place? I asked Thomas. "What we're really trying to do," he said simply, "is increase a person's confidence in being able to remember what he wants to remember and not remember what he doesn't want to remember, to increase his confidence in being able to control his memories."

That made sense. Feeling somewhat enlightened, I asked Thomas how he had gotten involved in the movement. He told me he was living in New York in 1950 when L. Ron Hubbard wrote a long article for *Astounding Science Fiction* called "Evolution of a Science." He read it, and then went out and bought a copy of Hubbard's magnum opus, *Dianetics: The Modern Science of Mental Health.* "It said," Thomas said, "do this and it'll happen, and I did it, and it happened." Somewhat modestly, he added, "And I've been impressed ever since."

I was right back where I had started, confused, absolutely unequipped to ask the right questions, the ones which would explain to me *what* happened, what Thomas meant. "Anybody," he was saying, "who seriously looks into Scientology rapidly gets over their misgivings. But there is always the sensational treatment in the press . . . the opprobrious use of the word 'cult,' which implies something secret. That is *wrong.* Scientology is open." That reminded me of something and I

asked him if he thought it would be all right for me to go to
the Scientology Congress coming up shortly. "You can go," he
said, "but I wouldn't make a big deal about being a reporter."
It was suddenly refreshing, hearing him say that, to see that
he was basically a realist, and quite sensitive to what the press
has reported about Scientology in the past. I had almost been
convinced they were genuinely above such secular concerns.

As I went down the hall from his small reception room to
get my coat, he said, "You come back yourself, will you?" He
meant that he wanted me to come back on my own, not on any
kind of an assignment, and find out what Scientology had for
me. I turned to thank him for the invitation. He was standing
in the light of the reception room, his arm raised, pointing
straight at me. It was almost a command, something ministerial in his stance, his head down slightly. It was uncomfortable and enveloping. It all became something more than
the few questions I had been sorting out in my mind. It became, all over again, a religion, a very mysterious religion. I
knew nothing.

I went to the Scientology Congress. The first person I talked
to there was a girl named Mary-Lou. She was tall and slender,
quite attractive, very much like many of the young girls deeply
involved in the movement. She had long brown hair and wore
long false eyelashes, which she tried not to flutter as she stared
into my eyes; being slightly nearsighted, her stare seemed even
more intense. We were in the main ballroom of the Hotel
Martinique. The Second Annual Eastern Scientology Congress
was presumably a festive occasion because a few balloons were
scotch-taped to the ceiling, several strands of wide crepe paper
festooned from corner to corner, and a large banner across
the front of the room proclaimed WELCOME CLASS VIII.
Behind me somebody said, "There are only thirty-five Class
VIII's on the planet." Most of the people there were young,
good-looking, smartly dressed, the girls in miniskirts, with

good long legs and bright open faces. The guys looked healthy, composed, some of them leaning to hippie-type open shirts and beads and long hair, others in smart semi-Edwardian suits. There were also quite a few older people, men in sports jackets and sports shirts that were buttoned up to the neck, elderly women sitting on wooden folding chairs as if to rest their tired feet, professional types wearing their overcoats and expressions of concentrated involvement, retired folk with tired faces and slight smiles. Somebody had patched WABC-FM into the loudspeaker system, and the tail end of the Beatles' "Hey, Jude" was blasting its interminable non-resolution over everything. It ended, finally, and on the same station—it was weird—some warm-voiced Latin type began singing "More." A girl sitting with a few friends began mouthing the words: *"More than the greatest love I've ever known. . . ."* There was this peculiar feeling in that room, not so much of unity, as of some kind of movement, not of being busy but of being fraternal, in *it* together, talking about this and that: your Grades, Straight Wire, Power, ARC, Successes! It all *felt* like movement, like action, but when you reached out for it, it just wasn't there.

Mary-Lou said she had been in Scientology for about a month and a half and it was just wonderful. Why, I asked her. What was she getting out of it? Freedom, she said, and I wondered if she had existed in some kind of bondage before Scientology. I asked her what she had done before. She just sort of shook her head. It was the same answer I would get from everybody I talked to. Before Scientology was a void, an emptiness nobody would discuss because it wasn't there. So I said, "Freedom?" to get her back to why she was in it. She smiled and nodded. "It brings out what's really me," she said with great sincerity. But, I pressed, didn't she know what she really was before? "Scientology tells you what you *really* are," she insisted, "and then shows you how to be it." I said nothing for a moment and she must have sensed a lack of enthusiasm, because she said, not in answer to any question, that in the past four months Scientology's enrollment had grown 500 percent. She didn't say she had been told that, or had heard it or read it; she *told* me. I asked if that was in terms of worldwide membership and she said she wasn't quite sure. I asked if it meant this country, or New York, and she said, twice, "I'm not really sure about that, I'm not really sure about that." So I said, "But it's grown five hundred percent. . . ." And she looked at me, struggling to maintain some kind of eye-lock which I suddenly understood was essential to people in Scientology, and said, "Yes, isn't that something?"

I thanked her—Scientologists thank each other incessantly to indicate communication has been achieved successfully—and turned to find myself looking up at the enormous, ever-present photograph of L. Ron Hubbard. For some reason, that first time, he made me think of a cross between H. L. Hunt and Len Deighton's General Midwinter, whose million-dollar brain was going to save the freedom-loving people of the world. "I got nothing against clichés, son. It's the quickest method of communication yet invented. . . ." Behind me a young man tapped on the microphone for our attention, and as people found seats and sat down, he explained that instead of the scheduled lecture we would hear a brand new tape from "Ron."

Everyone grew quiet with that uncomfortable rustle of not being quite ready to give full attention. The young man switched on a tape recorder and left the platform. There was some continued shuffling in and out of the ballroom and I began to wonder if everybody might not make a slow, unobtrusive exodus during the speech, seeing as how the tape recorder could not possibly feel offended. I was wrong. Though there was a steady in and out at the door, more people came in than left, and by the time somebody on the tape finished introducing Hubbard to what was obviously an audience somewhere else, the applause which met him where *he* was was joined by warm applause where I was. That was spooky. It was certainly a sign of respect for Hubbard, but let's face it, there was nobody there, just this tape recorder with its slowly turning reels, and Hubbard's even, somewhat mellow disembodied voice coming out of it. His topic was "Scientology: The Future of Western Civilization." He admitted it sounded presumptuous of him to bite off something like that, the notion that Scientology *was* the future of Western civilization. It was not at all presumptuous, he said, and launched into a long discourse on why man got to be the way he is. His talk touched on chaos-to-form or form-to-chaos, the latter being what history is *really* all about, the former what we are made to believe our path has been. The truth, he said, was that order—or form—preceded chaos, and it was man who was responsible for the chaos. He mentioned the obliteration of the individual, and how groups can be dangerous to the individual. He said war was government's attempt to do what taxes had failed to do; sustain confusion, I suppose. At one point, after a particular comment, he said, "You get the idea?" A voice behind me unhesitatingly answered, "Yeah!" Hubbard went on to say that there is no such thing as the masses, that the Communist powers—the commissars, as he called them with obvious relish—are fooling themselves when they talk about the greatest good for the greatest number of people. He pointed out that all troubles stem from individual aberrations; thus it is the solution of individual aberrations which will produce the salvation of Western civilization. It was a neat return to his major topic, from which he had ranged far and wide, rambling, cajoling, tossing off a few jokes which sent chuckles rippling through our audience while his, wherever he was, laughed heartily. Then he paused, and said, almost as a directive, "So introduce a little order, okay?" Two seats away from me, Mary-Lou and several other people said softly, almost in unison, "Okay."

Bob Thomas was in the reception room as I came out of the ballroom. He was smiling, tall, imposing; several people clustered around talking to him. He asked what I thought of the

Congress and I said I'd just heard the Hubbard tape. He looked around as several young girls walked by, all of them mod and very miniskirted, little bottoms sweet and round, and seemed about to say something. He caught himself, either because what he wanted to say might seem the kind of levity he wasn't used to revealing, or because he remembered I was writing about Scientology. I said goodbye to him and left. I was tired. In my mind, I tried to put some order into all I'd seen and heard. I remembered Mary-Lou telling me that Scientology's goal was to *clear* the planet within ten years. I suddenly understood that the ten years was from the *now* of her joining. There was no *fixed* date. It was a constant, a continuum, so that everybody who joins can tell themselves that, can give themselves the ultimate *raison d'être:* Ten years from today we will have saved the planet.

I was beginning to respect Scientology's ability to persuade. This was brought home to me even more tellingly when a very close friend told me why she involved herself with it. Her boy-friend had been in Scientology quite seriously, and when they began having problems, she agreed to go to several sessions to see if it might help them. "I never saw it as being a danger or anything like that," she told me. "It was a system. I wasn't sure it was a system I wanted to spend time on—I wasn't sure I wanted to spend time on *any* system investigating human functions. I was very passively involved, in that I wanted to work out my relationship with _____, and this was where he was working it out and it made sense to me to go to the same place. I remember at one point we had a really bad break and we thought we'd separate for good, and he was involved in Scientology at the time and through it it occurred to him we should try to work it out together. We stayed together another year. It had that much effect on our relationship."

Investigating Scientology, I was constantly confronted by my own feelings and convictions, my own doubts and fears.

Much of what I believed about people, about their wisdom and discretion, was challenged, as if I was reluctant to admit to myself that all of us—not only young people, whose lemming-like embrace of fads and fancies is so casually put down as just kids trying to be hip—are susceptible to movements such as Scientology which profess to have all the answers. My own skepticism was something I wanted to find in everyone, particularly in people already *in* Scientology. Some well-expressed doubts, I felt, would only enhance Scientology's validity. I only found unqualified enthusiasm, a determination to convince me of its enormous worth, and great efforts to get me to join. Everyone I talked to, particularly the kids trying to grab you with their eyes so that the electricity of their exuberance would crackle through to you, was only too eager to tell me about Scientology's various levels of "Release," and how they now feel "Marvelous!" and "Free!" And they were all advising me on the best way to get into Scientology: Take the Communications Course, you just *have* to take the Communications Course.

Why the Communications Course to start with? I asked a young girl at a Scientology branch office, 30 Fifth Avenue, where I had already been several times. This time I was there to buy some books, as well as a copy of Scientology's "Classification Gradation and Awareness Chart of Levels and Certificates." The girl was short, dark, plumpish, with thick legs that looked bad in the black English schoolgirl stockings and abbreviated wool miniskirt she was wearing. She said the reason everyone is encouraged to take the Communications Course is that it "helps establish the reality of Scientology." I must have looked puzzled, because she said it helps you understand the definition of things around you. You mean, I asked her, things we may have been seeing the wrong way? Her face lit up. "Yes," she said. "That's it!"

I nodded, and then asked if she could see about a copy of

the chart. I'd been to several branches and no one seemed to have any copies. She went into the small office just off the tiny area where stacks of Scientology's books were on display. I couldn't see who was in the office, but I heard a man's voice. I heard the girl ask him if I could buy a chart—he didn't see me or know who I was. I heard him, slightly incredulous, say, "Sure, if he wants one." As if to say, why not? sell it to him. He won't make head or tail of it.

His arrogance was exactly what I needed. Sure, the intentional mystery and complexity of Scientology was far from making sense to me, but after having visited this and other branches, I was getting some very strong feelings about the people in it; talking to them I knew I was beginning to touch the fringes of what it was all about.

My very first visit to the 30 Fifth Avenue branch had been to attend one of the small weekly parties Scientology throws to bring new people in, give them a chance to rap with the gang, buy a book or two, and maybe sign up for something. Almost the first thing I had asked about was whether or not Scientology is genuinely a religion, comparable to, say, Zen Buddhism? The people I talked to said that whereas religion is an abstraction, Scientology's strength lies in the fact that it is concrete, scientifically organized, and works. They all stressed that a lot, that it works. But why bother to call yourself a religion then, I pressed. A blond, crew-cutted fellow who sat behind the desk in the branch's small reception room sat back and said, "It's a religion only in that it's tax-free." He seemed to think that would satisfy whatever reservations I had about organized religion. I nodded, and then said, as if reminding myself what it was that put me off religions, that at some point, by necessity, to succeed, a religion becomes punishing. They—I think there were four of us now—quickly said that there was no element of that in Scientology. I remembered that later, when I was to read in a book called *Introduction to Scientology Ethics:* "There are four general classes of crimes and offenses in Scientology. These are ERRORS, MISDE-MEANORS, CRIMES AND HIGH CRIMES."

Oh, there is *discipline*. The blond fellow told me that when he didn't fulfill his "statistic," as he called it, a control was put on him which was in effect a penalty. He spoke in terms of five *chits*, and explained it was being penalized 5 or 10 per-cent of his salary for the week—the clear implication being that there is a quota system for everyone who works in Scien-tology. Exactly how it is measured I didn't know yet, but there was this quota system. At one point, explaining something about L. Ron Hubbard, he glanced over his right shoulder and pointed, casually, the way you would point to a minor objet d'art as you strolled down the halls of the Louvre, to the obligatory 11 x 14 photograph of Hubbard, looking down upon us.

I should describe this particular branch office because it was typical of many of the offices I would eventually visit. The small room we were in, the reception room, had a desk, with an easy chair next to it. Two easy chairs sat opposite the desk, with a potted plant between them. The desk was set at an angle to the door, to face any visitors who came in through the front door, which led directly off 12th Street, just off Fifth Avenue. To my right—I was sitting in one of the two easy chairs facing the desk behind which the blond fellow was telling me that after eight years in the Navy he found Scien-tology to be much better organized than the Navy—to my right was a small room with the piles and piles of Scientology books arranged on a table. Next to this room was the "execu-tive" office of the branch. To my left was a hallway which led to several other rooms. In the hallway a wall had been made over into a large bulletin board. Most of the notices on it, be-sides a list of what a good Scientologist does, and a list of what a good Auditor does, and rules for the *Preclear*, were short little notes from people in Scientology called "Successes." Each is a small, heartfelt testimonial to Scientology: "My ability to communicate has increased greatly and people find me much more desirable to communicate with." "Life is really worth living. I appreciate everything Ron is doing more than ever. Everyone come on the Road to Clear and O.T. . . . IT'S FREEDOM." Each "Success" carries the name of the person making the testimonial and its date. They are all a little like those votive offerings you find at the shrines of saints in churches throughout Greece, those small silvered plaques depicting parts of the body, put up by people who have been restored to health; in gratitude, once healthy, they bring flowers to the particular plaque because their backache or foot ache or eye discomfort has miraculously disappeared.

Beyond the bulletin board, all by itself, was posted a copy of the Classification Gradation and Awareness Chart of Levels and Certificates. I was reading off such things as "Relief Release" and "O/W ARC Process Case Remedies," and it made absolutely no sense to me, when a young fellow began talking to me. He proudly showed me where he was on the chart, a Grade IV—"Ability Release," I read. "Moving Out Of Fixed Conditions and Gaining Abilities To Do New Things." "There are several Grade IV's around here," he was saying. Then he pointed to a woman who was sitting off to the side in one of the rooms talking to somebody. "She's an O.T.III," he said with enormous respect. An O.T., I learned eventually, was an *operating thetan*, the ultimate. This woman was at the third level of achieving that sublime state, where, if I understood the oblique references made to O.T., you would be revered and listened to, and would possess *incredible* abilities—being able to walk on water or something, yet wise enough to know that it was not necessary to walk on the water to prove you could do it.

The young Grade IV suddenly offered to give me a small demonstration of the first thing you get in the Communications Course. As he was leading me over to some chairs stacked against the wall, he told me the course cost twenty-five dollars.

Later, his girlfriend, a pretty little thing with blonde hair and thin-outlined eyes that were wide and friendly, told me, "It's twenty-five dollars for the Communications Course, and if you don't dig it, they refund it." So her boyfriend tried to give me a simple demonstration of what is called *Confrontation*. He set a chair opposite mine and sat down, and the point was we were to stare at each other. We were to sit there and dig each other, free of all the little things we let intrude when all we should be doing is *looking* at someone. I suppose the procedure could make people who don't *like* to do that overcome their resistance to it. I suppose I could even convince someone that not being able to stare comfortably at a person is a hang-up to get rid of. It all felt a trifle self-conscious-making and we soon gave up on each other.

Back in the reception room, the blond guy behind the desk was about to say something when a young English girl walked in. He saw her, greeted her, and said, "I want to get your Success right away."

The girl was surprised. "Already?" she asked. "I only finished my Grades last week."

"Yes," the boy said. "We want to get it as quickly as possible when somebody Releases."

Releases. Insights. The terminology was getting to me, this private language which made it all a very private world. The girl said, about herself, "We've been clearing up quite a few engrams, some minor ones. We've located one which we can see is going to be a bit of a problem." She seemed proud of that. She had a problem. Something to sink your teeth into. My own feeling was that if it was a matter of dredging up a cranky wisdom tooth which refused to budge, okay. But these so-called *engrams*, as used in the lexicon of Scientology, are episodes in your past which left deep impressions, no matter how you recorded the event, consciously or unconsciously. Confessing to some clown staring at the needle readings off a simple meter, a Wheatstone bridge setup, that you watched your older brother groping with Mom did not seem the most fortuitous way to nullify the effect of that particular moment. What the young English girl had said was additionally unpleasant because it smacked of the same kind of blithe, guileless simplicity I used to run across in behavioral psychology textbooks. I prefer complexity. Rats in a maze, I believed somewhat naïvely, isn't you and me, Charlie.

I couldn't help but compare the outright blandness of the girl's "We've located one which we can see is going to be a bit of a problem" to the wrenching confession which confronts you in the unforgettable documentary film *Warrendale*. One of the children at Warrendale, the school for the emotionally disturbed, a girl, beautiful, sublimely lovely, reaches into herself and manages to say to one of the attendants, a calm, caring woman, that what she fears most of all in the whole world is that she will never, ever get well! It is a moment so crushing, so absolutely crushing, I shall never forget it. You not only are made to absorb this fact within the context of the girl's emotional state, her illness, but in that moment, because of how we've watched her wake up and dress and eat and lose her temper and scream and cry and then speak, you *know* where that confession came from; you know and you finally love the infinite complexity and tragedy of this girl because she is truly *alive*.

My own suspicion that Scientology was dangerously simplistic was further strengthened when I began reading some of the inexhaustible number of Scientology books, almost all of them written by L. Ron Hubbard. All of them seem to be, in their body, somewhat like all the books that keep coming out on the subject of bridge: How To Bid, How To Lead, How To Be Dummy . . . they go on and on and on. Which makes sense because it sustains interest and inertia. It is, in fact, the simplest way to breathe life into the movement. Hubbard lives, the books say to us; he lives and he thinks and continues handing down the Word. Despite the fact that I already felt, firmly, that most of the Scientologists urging me to read the books had not necessarily done so themselves, I did, from cover to cover. It was a chilling task, both numbing and annoying. What it all got down to, what was drenched in complexity, was the following message: You Can Do It, Fella! All By Yourself! Alone! Because Your Mind Is A Perfect Machine! And . . . you *cannot fail*. That's the hooker. You *cannot fail*. I should say the phrase in hushed tones, with reverence, wondering whether my own material self is capable of absorbing the enormity of that concept. And Hubbard, possibly because of his early experience as a writer of action science fiction, eschews lower case and continually lets you have it with all-capitals firing. YOU CANNOT FAIL. Got that? YOU CANNOT FAIL . . . CANNOT . . . CANNOT . . . CANNOT.

That is one hell of a beautiful promise: attain the unattainable; it *is* accessible. That is so much more attractive than merely learning How To Win Friends & Influence People, or pepping yourself up by Thinking Positive, or even getting caught up in the passion of a fiery revival meeting and Standing Up For Christ. And as opposed to traditional religions which speak of *someday*, in Scientology it is . . . soon. But then reality seems to step in, clumps in, in the person of the franchised Scientology branch, with its office and auditing rooms—often converted maids' rooms, the whole place usually a converted apartment. And the thought crosses my mind that if, two thousand years from now, the followers of the infallible system known today as Scientology record their humble beginnings, will the detailed descriptions of their difficult origins include the surroundings of neat lower-Fifth Avenue apartments as well as seedy West Side apartments, where *Preclears* step through a kitchen to reach the auditing room, where bare floors and folding chairs and a lack of ventilation accompanied it all as this determined science of the mind stood up to make itself known. Will all that mean as much to people in two thousand years as did the simple caves of the early Christians—

a fetid, difficult, impossible sustaining of a faith which, because it represented a political alienation, was seen to be dangerous and therefore had to be eradicated? Is that what is missing from Scientology as a modern religion, a feeling held in common by its followers that there is something dangerous in the air, something antisocial, something which may push them and their beliefs to an ultimate risk?

Scientology has of course received a great deal of criticism, much of it serious and sincerely concerned with what Scientology's processing techniques might do to what is popularly called "mental health." *Life* magazine published a lengthy, extremely subjective piece written by Alan J. Levy who took Scientology processing up to and including Grade IV. "I have Hubbard to thank," he wrote, "for a true-life nightmare that gnawed at my family relationships and saddled me with a burden of guilt I've not yet been able to shed. . . . I explored some nooks and crannies of my own psyche that I wish to God had never been unearthed." I asked Bob Thomas what he thought of the article. He was of two minds. "There were," he said, "fortunately, a couple of redeeming features. You get the impression that here is a very vital, powerful, worldwide spiritual movement, in spite of the fact that it [Levy's article] is presented in a very kooky way." I hadn't found the piece at all kooky. What happened was that during the course of the processing, Levy relived the anguish of his father's death, feeling he was somehow personally responsible for an inadequate response to the tragedy. Then, at one level, he was made to isolate the date of what he remembered to be a particularly serious argument he had with his wife. With his auditor's help he fixed the date, Sunday, March 18, 1958. Later, beginning to suffer severe headaches, he discovered that March 18, 1958, had been a Tuesday. He felt, he wrote, that he had been made to believe something which was simply not the truth. To this, Thomas said, "He tried to fool the meter—" Levy had not mentioned he was researching a piece for *Life* at any time while being audited by someone using Scientology's E-meter—"which *always* gives you a headache. We could've told him that." Thomas laughed. I asked what might have happened if Levy had said he was working for *Life* magazine. Rather than suggest Levy then might not have been allowed to continue, Thomas said, "He would've continued to have the insights that he relates having had. But it [the lie] caught up to him. Actually," he added, "his insights there are quite typical, quite classic, as a matter of fact, up to the point where his basic withholding of himself from full participation catches up to him. He couldn't fully participate because he was unwilling to really present himself as he was, fully. It's like going to a doctor, or going to a dentist to have a tooth pulled, and telling him it's *this* tooth, not the real one that hurts. So he pulls the one that doesn't hurt and you've still got the one that does hurt." As if I wasn't beginning to think so myself, Thomas said, "These techniques are very powerful, and when you go into a situation on a dishonest basis to begin with they can be shattering only because you're using something that's very powerful and direct, at the wrong targets, and you're not really participating validly. Not telling about being a reporter is a 'basic withhold.' Which, in terms of our technology of the reactive mind, activates the reactive mind. If you withhold something, it tends to reactivate the charge in the reactive mind. That's why we insist on no 'withholds,' on a very high degree of honesty. So if you have the finagle factor involved at the outset of the thing, no wonder it didn't go well. I'm surprised it went as well as it did. But the undeniable impression you get as you read his accounts of the processing is that something happened, he had some insights, in spite of the fact that he wasn't really there to do that."

I was impressed with what Levy had tried to do. He had put himself on the line to learn the facts. Feeling what I did about Scientology, his experience only made me more uncomfortable, and I wondered if there was a way to *experience* the whole thing without getting trapped. I encouraged myself by telling myself that many of the young people I had met were in it only because it was the Now thing to be in. I saw an invisible joyless quality to Scientology which would eventually discourage some of the younger people who were looking for excitement and entertainment. The weekly party at 30 Fifth Avenue was particularly typical to me. No one there was ever on any kind of a defensive when I pressed them about Scientology, but there was a blandness and an atmosphere which resolved itself, finally, into a kind of desultory joy. There was openness, but there was also a little boredom. I thought in particular of the little blonde and her Grade IV boyfriend. For her I knew it was all a social gathering and she would one day get tired and cut out. She had been in Scientology only a month and a half and must have joined because of the boy. She probably walked in one day, found him there, and stayed. For the moment, Scientology was happening. She was the one to first tell me about the celebrities getting into it. *"Jim Morrison,"* she said, and rolled her eyes. "I mean, that's what they say . . . but *then*—Wow!" What she was trying to say was that it *may* have been true—Scientology was not above using names to enhance its image—but if it was true . . . wow! What I felt in that branch office was that all of them, all the good-looking kids who permeate Scientology and give it a well-scrubbed gloss which is enormously advantageous, believe in Scientology. Up to a critical point, a point I sensed instinctively rather than saw. And then they either became members of the staff and accepted a few hard realities, like the risk of not producing and being docked a few *chits,* or they suddenly realized they were beginning to lead double lives: they talked about how honest and direct and responsible and *able* they were, but then you see them begin to exchange small looks which you've seen somewhere else—an uncertainty about appearing totally involved, at ease, or *at cause,* as Scientology calls it. An ego thing, as someone was to call it much later.

Is it all that *real?* is what they seem to be asking each other with their eyes.

One incident in particular made it all come to life and showed me something of the quality of the belief these young people had. The little blonde girl sat down across from her Grade IV and they began to stare at each other. It went on for a long long time, and suddenly it was like being back in high school, at some dance or party, where you've run out of things to talk about, dances to dance, risks to take, dreams to dream, and you unexpectedly find yourself in a staring contest with your date, and that contest becomes the most important thing in the world, and you stare and stare and stare, and just before you lose it, just before it goes, you suddenly wonder, my God, what is it I'm supposed to see there in her eyes? Isn't this just a simple exercise of wills? That was the innocence I began to feel about all of them, a wonderful, loving innocence of being able to survive a test of wills, as well as a test of what they were convinced they could bring out of themselves. The individual has become preeminent, and there is no such thing as mediocrity. We are all important. We all count. Someone named L. Ron Hubbard is telling us incessantly that we not only count, but count in superlatives. Yes, it is so very much like a test of wills, but in that, it becomes a small act of faith.

In the best writings about faith, and the problems of faith, what is ultimately most moving and affecting is that at a certain point all cant and ritual are torn away, all the beauty and solemnity and mystery of a church are done away with, and the individual finds himself confronted with his own capacity to *believe*. L. Ron Hubbard seems to appeal to the other side of that coin, to the idea that one needn't risk believing in an abstraction which may some day capriciously break his heart when, by using a very complicated and tinkertoy-like set of sophisticated steps, he can achieve pure rationale. What troubled me was that Hubbard was receiving more than undivided attention from the people in Scientology. He had their faith. That was why I felt a small sense of betrayal as I continued to investigate Scientology. When I spoke to people whose beliefs I was trying to assemble so that I could *grasp* it, my very questioning was a form of attack. But Scientologists do have trust in the system, and by virtue of trusting their system they, seeing me among them, trusted me. It was disarming.

If I was ever to understand Scientology for whatever it is, genuinely a religion, or a lesser social movement, or just a "cult," I had to begin with the man who had made it all come to life, Lafayette Ronald Hubbard. "Ron."

# "RON"

To most people in Scientology, Lafayette Ronald Hubbard is accessible only as a disembodied voice on a reel of tape, or as the source of a never-ending stream of books, pamphlets, mimeographed bulletins and directives, or as somebody they once saw on film, seated behind a large desk, patiently answering questions about Scientology. The man they see in the film wears an open-necked shirt and exudes a sense of enormous self-confidence, tempered with a certain joviality and homeyness. He is sleek and sure, with the suggestion of something once robust, totally in command, snatching at random, as he speaks, for simple analogies with which to prove a point, unexpectedly somber at the thought of man's inability to see what existence is all about. The voice itself is rich, with a kind of Don McNeill rolling of the "r's," and careful enunciation of words which are particularly telling to the comprehension of a particular thought. Where once, according to once-intimate acquaintances, there was an immediate sense of sheer power, of a "very big" man, with "tremendous" even "fantastic charm," not unlike *Henry VIII*, a man with "a powerful mind," and "a bit cynical," there is now calm and control and something very patriarchal.

Today, living in semimystical isolation on a converted ex-cattle boat in the Mediterranean, L. Ron Hubbard has, with characteristic grandeur, officially retired from the public arena, having withdrawn to his secular seclusion for the purpose of continuing his "studies and researches."

Assembling the facts of Hubbard's personal history was extremely difficult because whatever information I was able to unearth carried within itself seeds of its own contradiction. For example, references to places and events were written to imply that Hubbard had been on the spot without coming right out and saying unequivocally that L. Ron Hubbard had, on such and such a date, been *there* and done *this,* and if you wish you can quickly verify this by checking *The New York Times Index,* or *Who's Who,* or *The Encyclopaedia Britannica,* or . . . *something.* As a result, I began to wonder whether information given was always accurate, or whether one made conclusions about the man which were based on vague comments he might once have dropped, and had not disputed when they crept into print, as if to help create that aura of being shrouded in that charismatic vagueness obligatory to all men of vision. The technique of implication which Hubbard used—and continues to use—is clearly evident in the following, which he wrote in his book *Dianetics: The Evolution of a Science:*

> I remember one time learning Igoroti, an Eastern primitive language, in a single night. I sat up by kerosene lantern and took a list of words that had been made by an old missionary in the hills of Luzon—the Igorot had a very simple language. This missionary had phoneticised their language and he had made a list of their main words and their usage and grammar. And I remember sitting up under a mosquito net with the mosquitoes hungrily chomping their beaks just outside the net, and learning this language—three hundred words—just memorizing these words and what they meant. And the next day I started to get them in line and align them with people, and was speaking Igoroti in a very short time.

I don't dispute that Hubbard did find himself at some point in the Philippines. This was more than confirmed for me when I talked to Jack Horner, who for many years had been if not the most dedicated of Scientologists, then certainly among the first and the most faithful. Now working and living in Chicago, where he is an actor and free-lance writer and is developing his own system of thought which he is calling "Dianology," Horner told me: "I have a very parallel background to Hubbard: My father was in the Navy, my father was from Montana, I grew up for part of my childhood in the Orient. Hubbard and I even swam in the same swimming pool, only at different times; in Cavite, in the Philippine Islands. Near Manila, before World War II, there were some large naval bases, and there was a town called Cavite, which was right near Manila. And the Cavite swimming pool had salt water, and Hubbard and I got to discussing this one day and realized we had actually swum in the same swimming pools out there." This is the kind of tantalizing reference which is continually being fleshed out to form a substantial element in L. Ron Hubbard's past. Nothing is ever absolutely precise, and we are never sure when and under what circumstances he did something or went someplace. And it is all cloaked in a kind of prophet's discontent.

Hubbard was in the U.S. Navy. That is certain. And he was raised for some years of his life in Montana, on the cattle ranch owned by his maternal grandfather. He was born on March 13, 1911, in Tilden, Nebraska. His father was Commander H. R. Hubbard, U.S.N., and his mother was Ledora May Hubbard née Waterbury. But even these few bedrock facts may be open to question. When I was talking to Horner, he suddenly said, "By the way, if you want to check his birthplace and birth date, you will find there is no record." You mean, I said, in Tilden, Nebraska? "Yep," Horner said. Well, I asked, where was Hubbard born? "I don't know," Horner said. "But you won't find any records there." Is it true, I asked further, that Hubbard's father was in the Navy? "Yes," Horner said, "though I'm not sure whether that was his father or his stepfather. His [Hubbard's] son told me that years ago, and then recently somebody doing research tried to find a record of his birth in

Tilden and couldn't." Regarding Ron Hubbard's own military career, Horner said, "I'm sure he was in the Navy, but I'm sure a lot of the things he said happened in the Navy didn't."

Assuming Hubbard's father was his true father, the family was Scottish on the father's side and came to this country in the nineteenth century. Hubbard has embellished these bare bones by claiming other ancestry as well, particularly a Count de Loup, "who entered England with the Norman invasion and became the founder of the English de Wolfe family which emigrated to America in the seventeenth century." This is an attractive, even thrilling, notion, but in all fairness to the Almanach de Gotha, I must mention that in one of Hubbard's science-fiction adventures, he created a character named Mike de Wolfe—de Wolfe being the anglicized version of de Loup— who found himself back in 1640 as Miguel Saint Raoul Maria Gonzales Sebastian de Mendoza y Toledo Francisco Juan Tomaso Guerrero de Brazo y Leon de Lobo. De Lobo is Spanish for de Loup, which is French for . . . de Wolfe. Which inspired which?

Hubbard lived on his grandfather's Montana ranch until he was ten. A brief biography which appeared in *Scientology: The Field Staff Magazine,* written in a declamatory style which was to become increasingly familiar to me, said that he "could ride before he could walk," and "later became a blood brother of the Blackfeet (Pikuni) Indians, and his first novel, published in 1936, concerns them." The reference is probably to *Buckskin Brigade,* which appeared in hardcover in 1937.

Hubbard left Montana to rejoin his family, and when he was twelve was living in Washington, D.C., where Calvin Coolidge, Jr., was supposedly one of his best friends. The sudden death of the President's young son was supposed to have inspired Hubbard's "early interest in mental research."

The biography I'm quoting goes on to relate that when Hubbard was fourteen years old, his father was sent to the Far East, and it was not long before the boy found himself in

China, spending the next few years traveling throughout Asia. In northern China and India, the anonymous biographer explains, "he became intensely curious about the composition and destiny of Man, and studied on the one hand with Lama Priests, and made himself agreeable on the other hand to warlike people by his ability to ride." In 1930, this biography continues, Hubbard returned to Washington, D.C., and was enrolled at George Washington University. I found, however, that Hubbard had attended Helena High School in Helena, Montana, and had then come to Washington, D.C., where, in June of 1930, he graduated from Woodward School for Boys, a YMCA preparatory school. When, I asked myself, did he travel throughout Asia?

Hubbard's career at George Washington University is important because many of his researches and published conclusions have been supported by his claims to be not only a graduate engineer, but "a member of the first United States course in formal education in what is called today nuclear physics." The facts are that Hubbard never received a Bachelor of Science degree in civil engineering. He flunked freshman physics, was placed on probation in September of 1931, and failed to return to the university after the 1931-32 academic year. In later years, in addition to the "C.E." which he allowed to appear after his name, he added a "Ph.D." It eventually came out that the degree had been "granted" by Sequoia University, a nonaccredited California institution with the reputation of being something of a diploma mill.

The inhospitable memories of academic life did not seem to dim Hubbard's ravenous curiosities and zest for adventure. The biography in question states that upon leaving college, whenever that might have been, he led an expedition into Central America. "In the next few years he headed three further expeditions, all of them undertaken to study savage peoples and cultures to provide material for his articles and stories. Between 1933 and 1941 he visited many barbaric cultures and yet found time to write seven million words of published fact and fiction."

Put this all together and you have very few facts about the first thirty years of the man's life. I was very lucky to stumble across a zippy little profile which appeared in the July 1934 issue of a West Coast magazine called *The Pilot*, "The Magazine for Aviation Personnel," which threw a bit more light on Hubbard's youth. "Whenever two or three pilots are gathered together around the Nation's Capital," the column's author, one H. Latana Lewis II, wrote, "whether it be a Congressional hearing or just in the back of some hangar, you'll probably hear the name of L. Ron Hubbard mentioned, accompanied by such adjectives as 'crazy,' 'wild,' and 'dizzy.' For the flaming-haired pilot hit the city like a tornado a few years ago and made women scream and strong men weep by his aerial antics."

The colorful little sketch goes on to tell how Hubbard— "(also known as 'Flash')"—had stayed out west only long enough to be born, that he had then traveled all over the world, and eventually "fell from grace and became an aviator." Lewis reveals that Hubbard had already been, by the tender age of twenty-three, "a top sergeant in the Marines, radio crooner, newspaper reporter, gold miner in the West Indies, and movie director-explorer, having led a motion picture expedition into the south seas aboard an ancient windjammer." Hubbard then turned to flying a glider and became so proficient and fearless that he could make a sailplane perform stunts which brought "undertakers . . . out to the field. . . ." Lewis gives a brief, vivid account of one day in Chicago when "Flash" took up a glider and kept it aloft so long sailing on the heat waves rising from the baked tarmac that he set some record "for sustained flight over the same field."

Turning to power planes, the amazing Hubbard is credited with soloing his first time in a prop-driven craft, and quickly began to barnstorm around the country, flying "under every telephone wire in the Middle West." The piece concludes by saying that "after being one of aviation's most distinguished hell-raisers, he finally settled down with great dignity and became director of the flying club at George Washington University. And to make his taming complete, he took unto himself a co-pilot, a very wise and charming little aviatrix, whom Ron refers to as 'the skipper.' At present," the piece ends, "our young hero is buzzing around on the West Coast, where he writes magazine stories between flights. His playboy days over, he is now recognized as one of the outstanding glider pilots in the country."

The whole question of exactly how many expeditions Hubbard actually led into the uncharted wastes of Central America when he was not buzzing cows and hopping hedges from coast to coast is left unanswered. It is a fact that in 1940—not 1936 as his Scientology biography asserts—he was duly elected a member of the august Explorer's Club in New York. On his application, which Ward Randol, the club's executive director, refused to let me see because it was against policy, Hubbard wrote that since 1931 he had supported himself as a writer, specializing in adventure, with an output over the nine years of four million words.* In explaining the circumstances of Hubbard's election to the club, Mr. Randol told me in no uncertain terms that he personally knew the members who had sponsored Hubbard and certainly does not hesitate to vouch for their integrity and judgment. What is more, Randol was quite ready to reveal, in 1940 Hubbard made his first expedition as a member of the Explorer's Club, and was granted the club flag to carry on his voyage, a distinct honor given only when a member's application and description of an intended expedition has been given the severest scrutiny. "It's easier to

* This business of how many words Hubbard has actually written and had published insinuates itself perpetually though unobtrusively and manages to play a continuing role in reaffirming the substantiality of his labors. The figure also fluctuates enormously.

get money from us," Randol said drily, "than it is to get the flag. The flag is awarded only to members, and is treated rather jealously." Hubbard's expedition that year was to Alaska, under the title of the Alaskan-Radio Expedition. In the years since, Hubbard has made two more voyages flying the Explorer's Club flag, one in 1961, an Oceanographic-Archeological Expedition, and one in 1966, the Hubbard Geological Survey Expedition.

Much earlier, by 1941, American science-fiction fans were already familiar with Hubbard's distinctive writing style, which was bold and highly imaginative. His first serials began to appear in a pulp magazine called *Astounding Science Fiction* in 1938. One after another, titles such as *Slaves of Sleep, Kingslayer, Typewriter in the Sky, Fear, Death's Deputy,* and *Final Blackout* were eagerly welcomed by devoted fans. In addition to his own name, Hubbard also wrote under a variety of pen names, including René Lafayette (whose work appeared in such magazines as *Thrilling Wonder Stories* and *Startling*), Winchester Remington Colt, and, I suspect, some of the peripheral characters with names such as Jules Montcalm and Kurt von Rachne who popped up in his stories.

Moments in some of his sagas are particularly interesting because they offer insights into the workings of Hubbard's sense of fantasy, an imagination which was to achieve its full flower years later in Scientology. *Typewriter in the Sky* was the story of one Mike de Wolfe, who found himself trapped in the past as the unwilling villain of a swashbuckling tale being churned out by a science-fiction writer named Horace Hackett. How it happened never quite makes sense to Mike, but "he had no doubt that this was 'Blood and Loot,' by Horace Hackett, and that the whole panorama was activated only by Horace Hackett's mind. And what Horace Hackett said was so, was so. And what Horace Hackett said people said, they said." Mike eventually survived what he suspected was going to be a nasty finish, not because Horace Hackett wanted him dead, but because he knew how Horace's prolific mind resolved his melodramas. The end of the book finds Mike miraculously back in New York, at first grateful to have survived, thinking of seeing all of his old friends again. Then, remembering how he had wandered into Hackett's bathroom only to hear a typewriter begin to type and have everything disappear, only to awaken on a beach in the year 1640, Mike grows furious. It was Horace who had been responsible for the fate he had suffered, the killing of men he did not know, the falling in love with a woman he knew could never be his because she was just one of Hackett's creations. And then . . . "Abruptly Mike de Wolfe stopped. His jaw slackened a trifle and his hand went up to his mouth to cover it. His eyes were fixed upon the fleecy clouds which scurried across the moon.

Up there—
God?
In a dirty bathrobe?"

In a novella entitled *Fear*, Hubbard told of James Lowry, an ethnologist particularly fascinated by the notion of demonology in modern society, who, in what can only be described as a moment of blind jealousy, murders his wife and best friend, and then blanks out, growing steadily convinced that he is being secretly controlled by actual demons for reasons which he cannot understand. At one point in the story he hotly defends an article he has written on his favorite subject. "I have sought," Lowry argues, "to show that demons and devils were invented to allow some cunning member of the tribe to gain control of his fellows by the process of inventing something for them to fear and then offering to act as interpreter—"

Much later, just before everything falls back into some kind of order in his mind and he realizes what he has done, Lowry actually confronts what he knows to be his demons. They have told him he is the "Entity."

"You are the Entity, the center of control. Usually all life, at fleeting instants, takes turns in passing this along. Now perhaps you have, at one time in your life, had a sudden feeling, 'I am I'? Well, that awareness of yourself is akin to what men call godliness. For an instant nearly every living thing in this world has been the one Entity, the focal point for all life. It is like a torch being passed from hand to hand. Usually innocent little children such as myself are invested [the *demon* has appeared in the guise of a four-year-old girl with blonde locks, bow lips, and lewd eyes] and so it is that a child ponders much upon his identity."

Lowry does not seem to understand completely. The *demon* explains. "So long as you live, then the world is animated. So long as you walk and hear and see, the world goes forward. In your immediate vicinity, you understand, all life is concentrating upon demonstrating that it is alive. It is not. Others are only props for you. . . . You are the Entity, the only living thing in this world."

Gripping and inventive, the story is interesting because Hubbard later uses this idea of man's capacity to realize his godlike "Entity" in some of Scientology's fundamental beliefs and theories.

World War II found Hubbard an officer in the U.S. Navy, commissioned, according to the Scientology biography, before Pearl Harbor. "He was ordered to the Philippines at the outbreak of the war and was flown home in the late spring of 1942 as the first U.S. returned casualty from the Far East." What his wounds were is unknown, but he was in sufficiently good trim to be ordered at once to take command of a corvette, this due, it is said, to his considerable experience with small boats. He spent most of 1942 with his corvette and with the British and American antisubmarine vessels of the North Atlantic, rising to command an entire squadron. In 1943 he was back in the Pacific. No mention is made of the name of the ship he served on, in which campaigns, and in what capacity, but Hubbard has said on several occasions that it was he who provided Thomas Heggen with the model for "Mr. Roberts." This has never been substantiated. Heggen, before his untimely death in 1949, would only say about Roberts: "He is too good to be true, he is a pure invention."

When the war was over, Hubbard, to continue quoting his revealing, anonymously authored, and totally unsubstantiated biography, was "crippled and blind. . . . He resumed his studies of philosophy," this document goes on, "and by his discoveries so fully recovered that he was reclassified in 1949 for full combat duty. It is a matter of medical record that he has twice been pronounced dead and that in 1950 he was given a perfect score on mental and physical fitness reports. . . . Revolted by war and Man's inhumanity to Man, he resigned his commission rather than assist government research projects." With due respect to Hubbard's personal feelings of revulsion for war and man's inhumanity to man, I was unable to confirm a single one of these critical claims: that he had been crippled and blind, the nature of his "discoveries," and the medical records stating he had "twice been pronounced dead."

I flew to Washington, D.C., and learned that the United States Navy would not confirm or deny the details of Hubbard's military career.

"The records of members and former members of the armed forces," I was told in an official letter from the Department of the Navy, "are privileged in nature and information therefrom cannot be furnished without the written consent of the person whose records are concerned." I was able to learn, in conversations I had when I was in Washington, that Hubbard had been commissioned before the war broke out, that his rank during his military service was that of lieutenant, and that his classification or specialty was DVS, something called Deck Volunteer Specialist, if I understood the designation correctly. It also seems he did spend some time in a military hospital.

Several ex-Scientologists have told me that Hubbard was an outpatient while in the Navy, and that he felt free to roam around the grounds and wards and make friends with various patients, particularly those with psychological disturbances. It may be one of those apocryphal tales which only serves to cement the notion of already-developing wisdom and insight, but I think it is essentially true. Gary Watkins, a young man who had been a highly placed auditor * in Scientology at the time of being expelled by the movement, says that Hubbard, in the hospital, would talk to various patients. "He had lots of doubts about the theory [theories of mental illnesses] and would run off and find out what they knew—the experts in the books—about these patients and their cases, and then probably made his own extensions on that, and would sort of meet them casually in the garden and try to treat them."

After the war, according to an article in the *Saturday Evening Post* in 1964, Hubbard "banged around L.A. and Pasadena, where he was known as a fellow of an intense curiosity." Hubbard himself says that he first went to Hollywood as a screenwriter in 1936. This may be so, but the only screenplay which can be directly attributed to him is a fifteen-episode serial made by Columbia Pictures called *The Secret of Treasure Island*. I could find no mention anywhere of what happened to his wife, "the skipper," as Hubbard had called her, though he was, by the end of the war, the father of two children, a son, L. Ron Hubbard, Jr., nicknamed "Nibs," now working for a home protection agency in the Pacific Northwest, and a daughter, Kay. Hubbard himself has said only that his first wife died.

Whatever the facts may be, Hubbard was certainly a man of nervous versatility. Yet the wandering glider pilot and small-boats mariner who once sang and played the banjo on a radio program in California seemed gripped, in his various stories, by a genuine determination to explore the helplessness of man

---

* Scientology's own official definition of an auditor is: "A listener or one who listens carefully to what people have to say. An auditor is a person trained and qualified in applying Scientology processes to others for their betterment." The application of Scientology processes is called auditing, and will be defined and examined at length later.

as he inhabits his body, of being constricted by his own shell and thus unable to discover the higher meanings of existence. In one tale, *Death's Deputy*, the story of a fighter pilot chosen by Death to lead a charmed life which magnetically surrounds itself with tragedy after tragedy to create a source of supply for Death, the ill-fated hero is led to meet Death by a messenger who, when the pilot unconsciously touches his collar and finds no flesh there, says, "Don't be a fool. Does a man have to drag a body everywhere?"

So it was the *mind* of man which fascinated Hubbard, and his biography emphasizes that life and travel in Asia kindled the flame of this interest. Expeditions into savage wildernesses intensified his hunger for knowledge and resulted, in 1938, in the writing of a book which has never been published. Its subject, according to Hubbard, was "the basic principles of human existence." Its name: *Excalibur*. Like the steel of its namesake, the title rings on the imagination. "Mr. Hubbard wrote this work in 1938," advertising copy announced in the early 1950's. "When four of the first fifteen people who read it went insane, Mr. Hubbard withdrew it and placed it in a vault where it has remained until now. Copies to selected readers only and then on signature. Released only on sworn statement not to permit other readers to read it. Contains data not to be released during Mr. Hubbard's stay on earth. The complete fast formula for clearing. The secret not even *Dianetics* disclosed. Facsimile of original, individually typed for manuscript buyer. Gold-bound and locked. Signed by author. Very limited. Per copy . . . $1,500."

Somewhat conflicting details about this phenomenal work were revealed in the July 1952 issue of *Science-Fiction Advertiser*, a sort of science-fiction newsletter published in Glendale, California. The article was written by a science-fiction devotee named Arthur J. Cox and related how, in 1948, Hubbard had told his fans about "dying" for eight minutes during an operation performed on him while in the Navy. According to Cox,

> Hubbard realized that, while he was dead, he had received a tremendous inspiration, a great Message which he must impart to others. He sat at his typewriter for six days and nights and nothing came out. Then, *Excalibur* emerged. *Excalibur* contains the basic metaphysical secrets of the universe. He sent it around to some publishers; they all hastily rejected it. . . . He locked it away in a bank vault. But then, later, he informed us that he would try publishing a "diluted" version of it. . . . *Dianetics*, I was recently told by a friend of Hubbard's, is based upon one chapter of *Excalibur*.

Whatever the price tag, *Excalibur* has actually inspired fans to try and buy it. Jack Horner told me of being with Hubbard in Phoenix, Arizona, in 1953, when Hubbard was living and lecturing there, "and some guy came to the door trying to buy it. Well, Hubbard sent the guy away—handled him—and then looked at me and Jim Pinkham, and smiled." The moment seemed right, so Horner, who had begun to wonder if *Excalibur* really exists, got up enough courage and asked Hubbard point-blank. "I don't really recall word for word what he said," Horner went on, "but he implied that *Excalibur* was something that had been put there to create interest."

"You mean Hubbard made the whole thing up?" I said, stunned. "*Excalibur* doesn't exist?"

"I do not believe it does," Horner said candidly. "I don't believe that such a book did or does exist." Not that Hubbard was incapable of sitting down and knocking out a book he would title *Excalibur*. He was always prolific, almost driven, and had once said to Horner, "Any writer who can't write forty thousand words a week is not worth his salt." To help you appreciate that claim, 40,000 words is somewhat more than half the size of the book you are reading at this moment.

Hubbard's innate sense of what creates *interest* was definitely falling into place in the late 1940's when he wrote something called *Original Thesis*. He peddled it unsuccessfully to several publishers, including Shasta, a Chicago house specializing in science fiction which had published some of his other works. It was when he changed the name of his thesis to *Dianetics* that things began to happen. Whatever fire had burned inside Lafayette Ronald Hubbard for thirty-eight years had now found the beginning of its ultimate outlet and form of expression. He was home. Or, put another way, he had begun to fulfill a promise he once made, according to Jack Horner, to well-known science-fiction writer A. E. Van Vogt. "One of these days," he supposedly said to Van Vogt before he had written *Dianetics*, "I'm going to come out with something that's going to make P.T. Barnum look like a piker."

Jack Horner grows almost nostalgic when he talks about Hubbard and their closeness—"about the same relationship, over the years, that Mr. Nixon had with Mr. Eisenhower when he was in office"—and the gol'darned *similarities*. "We grew up in fairly parallel lives," he said to me. "I lived all over the United States; I was in the Navy myself during World War II, I lied about my age to get in. And because of having lived in many countries and around in different places, I had a very definite sense of equality and of people. Just before Hubbard came out with *Dianetics*, I was saying to myself: 'Why do people remember what they remember? And why do they forget what they forget?' I was doing my own line of thinking on this whole thing when *Dianetics* came out. I read what it had to say and I was fascinated! I got hold of the damn book and I sat down and audited three people and Boy! it worked just like Hubbard said it would. I was familiar already with the techniques of Freud and Breuer and pretty well into the history of Western psychology, so I said, 'Gee, he may not have it *all*, but he sure got a good piece of it! Let's go!' I just dropped everything and got involved. I was a very hardheaded, pragmatic atheist at the time *Dianetics* came out. You talk to me about past lives, I was very skeptical. Because as far as I was concerned, you had one life to live and that was it; you better do what you could while you were living it. However, when I audited enough people, and all of a sudden they kept dropping into past lives without my having mentioned them or their having read any books—" Horner suddenly gave a long, machine-gun-like laugh, as if to break the tension of what he was about to profess to believe, "—you begin to wonder, you know?"

The substantial contradictions of fact regarding Hubbard's background seem suddenly unimportant, or, as novelist William S. Burroughs put it in an article called "Scientology Revisited," published in England in *Mayfair* magazine: "Mr. Hubbard's degrees and credentials seem hardly relevant. Dianetics and Scientology are his credentials and he needs no others."

I agree. Let's take a look at the credentials.

# ENTER DIANETICS

I can remember, back in 1950, a high school friend telling me about some new thing his mother was involved with. He said it was called "Dianetics" and made it possible for you to remember things which had happened to you when you were just a baby. Then he said—and it was hard to believe, coming from an intelligent, level-headed guy—that Dianetics could make you experience things which had happened to you *before* birth. Why would you want to do that, I wanted to know, know things which had happened before you were born? As I remember, he didn't seem to know. He showed me a copy of the book his mother was studying, *Dianetics: The Modern Science of Mental Health.*

Reading it recently, that moment came back to me, particularly the book's first sentence. If ever an opening sentence introduced a theme with matchless daring, it was Hubbard's declaration that "the creation of dianetics is a milestone for Man comparable to his discovery of fire and superior to his inventions of the wheel and arch."

What was Dianetics, a word manufactured from the Greek word *dianoua,* meaning thought? It was a science of the mind, "an exact science and its application is on the order of, but simpler than, engineering. Its axioms should not be confused with theories since they demonstrably exist as natural laws hitherto undiscovered." Hubbard said his new science was simpler than physics or chemistry but on a much higher level—

43

he called it an "echelon"—of usefulness. *"The hidden source of all psychosomatic ills and human aberration has been discovered and skills have been developed for their invariable cure* [italics his]."

To give us all some perspective with which to appreciate the magnitude of his discovery, Hubbard, after a synopsis, an introduction, and instructions on how to read the book—"read straight on through. . . . Treat it as an adventure"—began Chapter I as follows: "A science of mind is a goal which has engrossed thousands of generations of Man. Armies, dynasties and whole civilizations have perished for lack of it. Rome went to dust for the want of it. China swims in blood for the hope of it; and down in the arsenal is an atom bomb, its hopeful nose full-armed in ignorance of it."

Without in any way lessening the impact of the complete text, here is the essence of what Hubbard had found. He postulated that the mind consists of two parts: the analytical mind (what Freud called the "conscious"), which perceives, remembers, and reasons; and the reactive mind (what Freud called the "unconscious"), which neither remembers nor perceives, but simply records. Normally, the analytical (conscious) mind is dominant. But, according to Hubbard, injury or anesthesia or, more important, acute emotional shock or physical pain, can "switch off" the analytical mind. Then the reactive mind goes into operation. This reactive mind does not record memories, but what Hubbard termed *engrams*—complete sound impressions on protoplasm itself, "a complete recording," as he put it, "down to the last accurate detail, of every perception present in a moment of . . . unconsciousness." Unhappiness, emotional upsets, even the common cold, were caused by the existence of these engrams. Dianetics therefore was the discovery, study, and technology for dredging up these troublemakers and getting rid of them.

Probably the first man to learn something about Hubbard's discovery and immediately accept it was John Campbell, Jr., editor of *Astounding Science Fiction*, the magazine which had published many of Hubbard's stories and serials. Hubbard had explained his extensive theories and techniques to Campbell, and provided dramatic proof by alleviating Campbell's chronic sinusitis. Campbell was enormously impressed, so much so that he and Hubbard quickly established a Dianetics organization in Bay Head, New Jersey, a town not far from Elizabeth, New Jersey, where Campbell's magazine was headquartered. At the same time (this was July of 1949), Campbell wrote a long letter to Dr. Josephus Augustus Winter, a general practitioner from St. Joseph, Michigan, who had published several articles on medicine in *Astounding Science Fiction*, telling him all about Hubbard's investigations. "L. Ron Hubbard," Campbell wrote, "who happens to be an author, has been doing some psychological research. . . . He's gotten important results. His approach is, actually, based on some very early work of Freud's, some work of other men, and a lot of original research. He's not a professional psychoanalyst or psychiatrist . . . he's basically an engineer. He approached the problem of psychiatry from the heuristic viewpoint—to get results. . . ." Campbell went on to describe some of Hubbard's results, particularly the taking of an amputee veteran right through a period of unconsciousness to discover why he was feeling so troubled, why he thought there was nothing to live for.

When Dr. Winter, as he was later to describe it in his book, *A Doctor Looks At Dianetics*, wrote Campbell asking for more details of what, at first glance, certainly looked interesting, Campbell answered with another long letter that once more urged the doctor to come and see for himself, and then added, in substantiation of Hubbard's work: "He has one statistic. He has *cured every patient* [italics his] he worked. He has cured ulcers, arthritis, asthma." Winter found this blatant confidence almost too much to believe, but refused to dismiss Hubbard outright. Instead, he wrote directly to Hubbard, asking for even more details. Hubbard wrote back to say that he was "preparing, instead of a rambling letter, an operator's manual for your use. . . . Certainly appreciate your interest. My vanity hopes that you will secure credit for me for eleven years of unpaid research, but my humanity hopes above that that this science will be used as intelligently and extensively as possible, for it *is* a science and it does produce exact results uniformly and can, I think, be of benefit."

Dr. Winter arrived in Bay Head on October 1, 1949, and was quite impressed with Hubbard's theories and the few demonstrations he witnessed. His feelings, however, were not fully secured until after he had returned to St. Joseph, Michigan, to spend Thanksgiving with his family. There, when his little son's fear of ghosts became quite serious, Dr. Winter decided to try some of Hubbard's dianetic methods. When, with only a little assistance, the boy was able to describe accurately the moment of his own birth and the certainly frightening image of the white-masked doctor who had brought him into the world, Dr. Winter was forced to acknowledge that not only had he discovered his son's "ghosts," but L. Ron Hubbard's discovery appeared to be a working science precisely as claimed. Dr. Winter returned to Bay Head to continue his work with Campbell and Hubbard. After another short trip back to Michigan for Christmas, he decided he must devote all his energies to Dianetics. He closed his practice and, with his family, moved to Elizabeth, New Jersey, which was now Hubbard's headquarters. In April of 1950 the first Hubbard Dianetic Research Foundation was incorporated, with Dr. Winter as its first medical director.

The world at large, meanwhile, was only beginning to learn something of this revolutionary discovery. Under what Hubbard has described as enormous pressure from followers, he finally allowed John Campbell to publish, in May of 1950, in *Astounding Science Fiction,* an article called "Evolution of a Science." This caused great turmoil among science-fiction devotees and was followed, very quickly, with the appearance of the book, *Dianetics: The Modern Science of Mental Health.* Much to everyone's surprise, it became an immediate best seller, the first book to achieve such instant success since Thomas Merton's *The Seven Storey Mountain.* Though most of the reviews were adverse, people all over the country were not only buying the book, but enthusiastically organizing themselves into coven-like Dianetics groups eager to practice the phenomenal techniques Hubbard revealed in his tome. While sociologists dismissed the whole thing as just another American fad, more of that postwar hysteria which had produced pyramid clubs and canasta marathons, they could not pretend that everybody wasn't getting into it.

I have already mentioned that Hubbard had tried to sell the book under another title, *Original Thesis*—this was the volume he sent Dr. Winter, the "operator's manual" which inspired the doctor to go personally and see what Dianetics was all about. Naming his science "Dianetics" and then generating a great deal of talk through the *Astounding Science Fiction* article finally made the difference and put Dianetics on its feet. Hubbard himself has discussed the tortuous path he followed to develop his science, but not only in terms of hitting upon just the right name and achieving the right kind of exposure. "In a lifetime of wandering around," he wrote in the *Astounding* article, "The Evolution of a Science,"

> many strange things had been observed. The medicine men of the Goldi people of Manchuria, the shamans of North Borneo, Sioux medicine men, the cults of Los Angeles, and modern psychology. Amongst the people questioned about existence were a magician whose ancestors served in the court of Kublai Khan and a Hindu who could hypnotize cats. Dabbles had been made in mysticism, data had been studied from mythology to spiritualism. Odds and ends like these, countless odds and ends. . . . First, attempts were made to discover what school or system was workable. Freud did occasionally. So did Chinese acupuncture. So did magic healing crystals in Australia and miracle shrines in South America.

But eclectic as his bent was, the answers had to be worked out by Hubbard and Hubbard alone. After many long years of wrestling with these questions, he concluded that man, possessed of a brain which is in fact a miraculous, perfect computer, needs a *dynamic* (italics his) principle by which to examine his existence. With this firmly in mind, L. Ron Hubbard began to postulate, build, and conclude. In charting the hitherto unknown mysteries of man's true existence, he was constantly guided by one basic principle: "a science . . . is something pretty precise. . . . It has to produce predictable results uniformly and *every time* [italics his]." I must emphasize one thing here: in all the millions of words which followed the appearance of *Dianetics,* in all the contradictions and verbal gymnastics which have led followers into labyrinthine confusion as well as predetermined insights, Hubbard has managed to sustain his dedication to this one scientific notion of validity-through-workability with startling fidelity.

In moments of rare candor, Hubbard has boasted that it actually took him a mere three weeks to write the entire weighty text of the original Dianetics book. I don't doubt him. It is known that he wrote on a special IBM electric typewriter which had much-used words such as "the," "and," and "but" slugged in as entire keys. He also typed on a continuous roll of paper to avoid the interruptions of changing sheets.

However long it actually took Hubbard to write *Dianetics: The Modern Science of Mental Health,* the style of the book is diffuse, rambling, and repetitive, and very quickly introduces us to one of the basic characteristics of a new school of thought: its own vocabulary. Words such as *Anaten, Basic-Basic, Chains, Clear, Denyer, Perceptic,* and many more, peppered the writing, bringing a reader to a grinding halt as he stopped to ask himself exactly how Hubbard had chosen to employ a particular word. Hubbard justified his rampant neologism in a lengthy footnote—footnotes becoming an essential technique in everything he wrote. He explained that verbs and adjectives were being used as nouns because old terminology was useless in defining the elements of his new science. It was much simpler to invent language and give it mint-new definitions.

Dr. Winter's book, *A Doctor Looks At Dianetics*, threw more candid light on Hubbard's use of language. Winter said that when he and Hubbard and Campbell first developed the advanced aspects of Dianetics, organizing it and codifying its principles, "we concluded that terminology should be revised with the following criteria in mind: Older terminology or terminology from other medical fields should be avoided, because the acceptance of a term from a certain school of thought might imply acceptance of the tenets of that school of thought." Whenever possible, "we would coin a new term," so that Dianetics would possess its own validity, its own substantiation of its discoveries.* The usefulness of this tactic has been, through the years, reinforced by a small *Important Note* which appears as the frontispiece of virtually every book written on either Dianetics, or its successor, Scientology: "In studying Scientology (Dianetics) be very, very certain you never go past a word you do not fully understand. The only reason a person gives up a study or becomes confused or unable to learn is that he or she has gone past a word or phrase that was not understood. If the material becomes confusing or you can't seem to grasp it, there will be a word just earlier that you have not understood. Don't go any further, but go back to BEFORE you got into trouble, find the misunderstood word and get it defined."

---

* A curious exception to this neologism was the word *engram* itself. It had already been defined as a psychical change caused by some sort of stimulation in 1936, in the 17th Edition of Dorland's *Medical Dictionary*. Even earlier, in 1923, Richard Semon used the term in his book *Mnemic Psychology*. Dr. Winter hotly denied that the term had been lifted from the Semon book, though he acknowledged finding it in the Dorland.

Once we actually understand the definitions of Hubbard's analytical and reactive minds, we are introduced to the high drama of how engrams become implanted. Wrote Hubbard:

> A woman is knocked down by a blow. She is rendered "unconscious." She is kicked and told she is a faker, that she is no good, that she is always changing her mind. A chair is overturned in the process. A faucet is running in the kitchen. A car is passing in the street outside. The engram contains a running record of all these perceptions: sight, sound, tactile, taste, smell, organic sensation, kinetic sense, joint position, thirst record, etc. The engram would consist of the whole statement made to her when she was "unconscious": the voice tones and emotion in the voice, the sound and feel of the original and later blows, the tactile of the floor, the feel and sound of the chair overturning, the organic sensation of the blow, perhaps the taste of blood in her mouth or any other taste present there, the smell of the person attacking her and the smells in the room, the sound of the passing car's motor and tires, etc.

The intensity of an engram's moment of implantation was balanced by the delicate probing designed to dredge it up years later. Called auditing, it was performed when a person was in what was called *dianetic reverie,* a supposed partial sleep which simplified recalling an engram, bringing it up to the surface and, in the ever-expanding jargon of Dianetics, "boiling it off." The one engram dianetic auditors were determined to locate as quickly as possible was the one Hubbard named the *Basic-Basic,* or BB, which, Dianetics believed, was formed a few weeks after conception, or even earlier, in the zygote, the fertilized ovum. Tracing a BB was extremely sophisticated auditing, and one usually "ran" countless lesser engrams which had been experienced prior to the moment of birth before confronting this ultimate nemesis. That there were plenty of engrams to locate from the time of the formation of the embryo is argued convincingly by Hubbard in his description of life in the womb. "Mama sneezes," he wrote in

*Dianetics: The Modern Science of Mental Health,* "baby gets knocked 'unconscious.' Mama runs lightly and blithely into a table and baby gets its head stoved in. Mama has constipation and baby, in the anxious effort, gets squashed. Papa becomes passionate and baby has the sensation of being put into a running washing machine. Mama gets hysterical, baby gets an engram. Papa hits Mama, baby gets an engram. Junior bounces on Mama's lap, baby gets an engram. . . ."

There are also the noises, the incessant cacophony of the interior universe: "Intestinal squeaks and groans, flowing water, belches, flatulation and other body activities of the mother produce a continual sound. . . . When mother takes quinine a high ringing noise may come into being in the foetal ears as well as her own—a ringing which will carry through a person's whole life."

The techniques of auditing and locating engrams were made immeasurably simpler by Hubbard's strongly held conviction that there was one engram common to almost all of us. "What happens to a child in a womb?" he wrote rhetorically in "The Evolution of a Science." "The commonest events are accidents, illnesses—and *attempted abortions!* [italics and emphasis his] Call the last AA. Where do people get ulcers? In the womb, usually, AA. Full registry of all perceptics down to the last syllable, material which can be fully dramatized." Much as we would do, Hubbard asks the question which is on our minds. "How does the foetus heal up with all this damage?" His answer: "Ask a doctor about twenty years hence—I've got my hands full."

But what he was talking about was not just *one* attempted abortion: "Twenty or thirty abortion attempts are not uncommon in the abereee, and in every attempt the child could have been pierced through the body or brain." Pierced, because the AA is usually done with knitting needles. It is no wonder that he firmly believes these horrible experiences produce the worst possible engrams.

A large proportion of allegedly feeble-minded children are actually attempted abortion cases [he wrote] whose engrams place them in fear paralysis or regressive palsy and which command them not to grow but to be where they are forever.

Morning sickness [he writes further] is entirely engramic, so far as can be discovered. . . . And the act of vomiting because of pregnancy is via contagion of aberration. Actual illness generally results only when mother has been interfering with the child either by douches or knitting needles or some such thing.

If the husband uses language during coitus, every word of it is going to be engramic. If the mother is beaten by him, that beating and everything he says and that *she* says will become part of the engram. . . . A woman who is pregnant should be given every consideration. . . . *For every coital experience is an engram in the child during pregnancy* [italics his].

Hubbard's extensive discussion of things sexual, his concern with abortions, beatings, coitus under duress, flatulence which causes pressure on the foetus, certain cloacal references, all suggest to me a fascination which borders on the obsessive, as if he possessed a deep-seated hatred for women. All of them are being beaten, most of them prove to be unfaithful, few babies are wanted. According to everything he has written, however, Hubbard is merely trying to describe how man responds to threats, no matter what dramatic form they may take. Hubbard believes that man is motivated by the need to survive; he writes it in capitals, SURVIVE, and calls it his First Dynamic. To this he adds three more Dynamics, the urge to survive via the sexual act, the urge to survive as a group, and the urge to survive as Mankind.

During auditing, with a patient in *dianetic reverie*, there was a reported tendency to yawn and stretch, immediately interpreted as visible proof that the session was progressing successfully and engrams were being brought to the surface. Unexpected aches and pains also appeared mysteriously, and then disappeared just as mysteriously. These, Hubbard explained, were the lingering effects of psychosomatic ills which would never return. After the particular, long-sought-after engram was finally brought up and "boiled off," the patient had a sense of enormous relief, so intense that he often began to laugh uncontrollably. Dr. Winter reported that shortly after arriving at the Foundation in Elizabeth he was completely taken aback by the sight of a patient who had been extremely morose suddenly breaking out in laughter, not to stop for several hours. Hubbard brushed this off as being normal, and said there was one patient who had laughed for two days.

*Dianetics: The Modern Science of Mental Health* contains several vivid examples of auditing at work. At one point Hubbard described a technique he called the "repeater," and gave a vivid example of how it was used on a young girl who had resisted confronting her "basic area" for seventy-five hours. The technique involved the repeated use of what appears to be a key phrase in the person's life to take them back to that time, that "basic area" where trouble originated. The incident is reprinted in script form, with the auditor's and the girl's dialogue accompanied by parenthetical observations explaining what is happening and why. The auditor leads the girl, whom he (Hubbard) describes as being "very bored and uncooperative," back to where she suddenly feels a pain (somatic) in her face which grows stronger and stronger. Suddenly the girl hears a voice, her father's. The auditor asks her to repeat his words. The girl says he is talking to her mother, and complains of the pain, or pressure, on her face being uncomfortable. The auditor prompts her to repeat the words she hears. The girl says she hears her father telling her mother he won't "come in you now." As we realize the girl is remembering her parents having sexual intercourse while she was in her mother's womb, the girl is telling the auditor that the moment she recalled her father's voice, the pressure on her face became less. The auditor, patience personified according to the script, insists the girl stay there and repeat what her mother is saying. The girl says her mother is angry, and is telling her father she doesn't want him. "Say," the girl says at this point, "the somatic stopped." The parenthetic explanation is "(Coitus had ended at this point.)" The auditor then asks the girl to start all over again. She does, wonders what her parents are up to, realizes herself what is happening, and is momentarily embarrassed. The auditor calmly asks her to go through the event once again. She does so, in detail, recalling her father's words and then her mother's angry answer. The auditor insists on yet another repetition. This goes on until, according to Hubbard, the pain disappears completely. He ends the scene by saying that the girl "feels quite cheerful . . . but doesn't think to mention that she doubted prenatals existed."

According to Hubbard, it takes some twenty hours of auditing before a person who is aberrated becomes a "release," someone free of all major neuroses and ills. Hubbard calls it "a state superior to any produced by several years of psychoanalysis, since the release will not relapse." Beyond being a release lies becoming a *preclear* and finally a *clear*, someone completely free of engrams. "Clears," Hubbard explains, "do not get colds," their wounds heal quickly if injured, their eyes are keener, and their I.Q.'s visibly increased. "The dianetic clear," he put it quite simply, "is to the current normal individual as the current normal is to the severely insane." An auditor, the person responsible for bringing someone to this obviously desirable state, needed very little qualification to practice his ability. A careful reading of the original dianetic text was considered sufficient, though student auditors were strongly urged to go to Elizabeth, New Jersey, and take the professional course at the Foundation.

What with best-sellerdom and the extensive coffee-klatch practicing of dianetics techniques, L. Ron Hubbard, Dianetics, and the startling results it claimed received so much attention that it was inevitable that before too long, professional associations would take a closer look at his activities. The Hubbard Dianetic Research Foundation, Inc., had, early in the summer of 1950, made a presentation of Dianetics to a group of psychiatrists, educators, and lay people in Washington, D.C. It was the only genuine such presentation ever made, and Dr. Winter found it to be something of a failure.

> Some of the psychiatrists [he wrote in his book]—perhaps the more progressive and open-minded ones—had evinced an interest in the novel postulates and intriguing conclusions of dianetics. . . . I did not feel that the Washington venture was a successful one—at least, not from the medical point of view. It was noteworthy that most of the people whose interest in dianetics had been augmented by this presentation were members of the laity, rather than the profession, and I thought that I could detect in their attitudes the fervor of the convert, rather than the cool, objective interest of the scientist. The professional people evidenced an interest in the philosophy of dianetics; their interest was repelled, however, by the manner of presentation of the subject, especially the unwarranted implication that it was necessary to repudiate one's previous beliefs before accepting dianetics.

In September of 1950, the American Psychological Association called on psychologists not to use dianetic therapy, "in the public interest." Struggling to maintain circumspection, the Association unanimously adopted a resolution at the last session of a meeting of its council of representatives which stated that, "While suspending judgment concerning the eventual validity of the claims made by the author of 'Dianetics,' the association calls attention to the fact that these claims are not supported by empirical evidence of the sort required for the establishment of scientific generalizations. In the public interest, the association, in the absence of such evidence, recommends to its members that the use of the techniques peculiar to Dianetics be limited to scientific investigations designed to test the validity of the claims."

From Los Angeles, where he was lecturing and setting up

another Hubbard Dianetic Research Foundation, L. Ron Hubbard answered that he was ready to furnish proof of every claim made in his book. He went on to say that as long as a year earlier he had made such an offer to the American Psychological Association and had never heard from them. He said he had already submitted proof to several scientists and associations, and expressed total agreement with the notion that the public was entitled to proof. He said he was ready and willing to give it in detail. And then he made what I can only charitably call a tactical blunder.

Speaking to 6,000 people in the Los Angeles Shrine Auditorium, Hubbard introduced a girl named Sonya Bianca and said she was a *clear*, possessing total recall of all *perceptics* (sense perceptions) for her entire past, as well as kinetic abilities. It was a disaster. Miss Bianca not only could not remember basic formulas in physics, the subject she was supposedly majoring in, but could not give the color of Hubbard's tie when his back was turned, and certainly could not, exercising her kinetic powers, knock off somebody's hat at fifty feet. In a matter of minutes the audience was streaming out of the hall in moods ranging from gagging hilarity to plain disgust. But Hubbard, with a sense which suggested anticipation, explained the whole thing away as having been his fault. He had, he said, called Miss Bianca on stage by saying, "Will you come here *now*, Sonya?" and in doing so, using the "now," trapped her in present time.

At about the same time, the first cracks began to appear within the Hubbard Dianetic Research Foundation in Elizabeth. Dr. Winter was growing increasingly annoyed at Hubbard's authoritarian behavior and his flat refusal to use some semblance of a scientific approach—scientific in Dr. Winter's terms. In his lectures in California, Hubbard was already talking about something he called the *Theta*, and MEST (a conglomerate word created from the first letters of matter, energy, space, and time). There was also talk of doing away with *dianetic reverie* in auditing sessions and replacing it with something called an electropsychometer, a crude polygraph or lie detector developed by an inveterate West Coast gadgeteer named Volney Mathison. Rather than be in reverie, a person being audited would hold two cans connected to the small box which had a meter on it, and a minute current would be passed through the person's body, giving various readings on the meter as the person answered various questions. Dr. Winter, hearing these reports, grew increasingly apprehensive. Jack Horner, who was at the foundation taking the auditor's course, remembers the disagreements which flared between the two men, particularly with regard to the business of "past lives," which was offensive to Winter who was struggling for order and scientific neatness. Yet he was constantly being undermined. "There was a bulletin on the board," Horner tells, "which said: 'Any Student Running Past Lives Will Be Suspended.' So of course everybody started running past lives."

In October of 1950 Dr. Winter finally severed his relations with the Foundation and left to establish his own dianetic practice. The book he wrote soon after, *A Doctor Looks At Dianetics,* is revealing not only because of the way he openly criticizes Hubbard and some of his methods, but because Dr. Winter argues emphatically that there are valid and valuable aspects to Dianetics. To begin with, he strongly doubted that what Hubbard had called a patient's "sperm dream" actually occurred. He also disputed, rather critically, Hubbard's claim that anyone could be an auditor—Hubbard had once described a potential auditor as "any person who is intelligent and possessed of average persistency." Dr. Winter wrote that "something more than enthusiasm for a new idea was needed to make a good therapist." Finally, the doctor wondered aloud why he had never encountered anyone who was actually *Clear.* While he did support the principles of the existence of prenatal engrams, and the importance of precise methods for locating troubles whose cause was psychosomatic, he was completely put off and angered by the science-fiction elements of Hubbard's thinking.

At about the same time that Dr. Winter was leaving the New Jersey foundation, the flamboyant, totally confident Hubbard was already having problems with the board of his California Research Foundation, barely a few months old. Jack Horner had been sent to Los Angeles to help establish the training courses and remembers one incident when Hubbard summarily fired two men from the L.A. staff. "It seemed very unjust," Horner told me, "so I went to see him about it. You have to understand that I was only about twenty-one at the time." Brash, committed, and unafraid to face the boss. "I went to his office and I said, 'This is ridiculous. These people are not Communists!' And he paced up and down, and he said, 'Look, I've got a battle to fight. I may lose some people along the way, but I'm going to win the battle.'" If Hubbard meant the frictions between himself and the Los Angeles staff, and problems with Dr. Winter back in New Jersey, and mounting criticism from outsiders, then the battle had surely been joined.

In January of 1951, the New Jersey Board of Medical Examiners instituted proceedings against the Hubbard Dianetic Research Foundation, Inc., for conducting a school which, it was charged, was teaching medicine, surgery, and a method of treatment, without a license. The New Jersey operation quickly closed its doors, and Hubbard moved to Wichita, Kansas, where he incorporated another Hubbard Dianetic Research Foundation.

Despite all the movement and allegations and internal difficulties, the work of the foundation had by this time taken on a somewhat formal look. Both the West Coast and Wichita foundations offered a one-month professional Dianetics auditor's course for $500. There was a second course consisting of a series of fifteen lectures involving two teams which would "co-audit" each other. This course cost $200 per person or

$350 per team. A third course consisted of one two-hour session conducted by a "professional auditor" who would lead each member of a team through *dianetic reverie*—it was still being used—under the observation of the team member, the "co-auditor" in training. This course cost $15. In addition to the courses, the foundations advertised "associate" memberships in the Hubbard Dianetic Research Foundation. This entitled one to receive copies of *The Dianetic Auditor's Bulletin*, the foundation's official publication which told subscribers all about the latest developments in Dianetics. The "associate" membership cost $15 a year.

The public excitement and controversy generated by Dianetics at this time was matched by upheavals in Hubbard's personal life. He had married a second time, and in April of 1951, Sara Northrup Hubbard sued him for divorce, testifying that doctors had told her that her husband was suffering from "paranoid schizophrenia." She also charged that he had subjected her to "systematic torture" by beating and strangling her, and denying her sleep. The divorce was granted in June and gave Mrs. Hubbard custody of their fourteen-month-old son, Alexis, and $200 a month support. In a surprise move, however, it was Hubbard who actually won the divorce decree on a cross petition in which he charged gross neglect of duty on the part of Mrs. Hubbard. The ex-Mrs. Hubbard eventually remarried.

Meanwhile, Hubbard's relations with the Los Angeles Dianetic Foundation had deteriorated to such a point that he summarily broke with them that same year, 1951. The operation in Wichita was also doing badly and on February 21, 1952, filed a voluntary petition for bankruptcy. A Wichita businessman eventually bought it from the bankruptcy court, publicly announcing that he would have absolutely nothing to do with Hubbard. To anybody underestimating Hubbard's imagination and resilience, it seemed obvious that he was finished.

# SCIENTOLOGY

The more I learned about Hubbard the more fascinated I became to find how eagerly everybody kept *underrating* him. The reason, I guessed, was because we tend to give others much more credit for insight, objectivity, and personal self-confidence than we should.

Hubbard survived to succeed because enough people wanted him to succeed. At the same time, news stories about him and his activities have always been smugly snide, written in that almost traditional "God-forbid-we-should-give-the-crackpot-credence" style. Which is also understandable, except for the fact that a man like Hubbard *thrives* on being dismissed by the establishment. Late in 1952, *Time* magazine reported the appearance of Scientology, saying: "His [Hubbard's] latest ology is compounded of equal parts of science fiction, dianetics (with 'auditing,' 'preclears,' and engrams), and plain jabberwocky." The jabberwocky was substantiated by quoting from one of Hubbard's new books, *Scientology: 8-80*: "An individual who cannot get out of his body immediately can look around inside his head and find the black spots and turn them white. . . ."

I would be perfectly prepared to dismiss this sentence as utter nonsense, except that a sincere Scientologist I met during my inquiries told me, with no prompting or being brought around to the subject, that "the greatest thing was the day I suddenly looked inside my head and I turned the black spots white!" To me, this seemed more than a believer swallowing everything and *anything* the leader says; here was an apparently rational being demonstrating that he had been brought to a stage where he was capable of doing—to himself—that which L. Ron Hubbard said could be done. How the hell do you just dismiss that?

In the spring of 1952, Hubbard resigned from the bankrupt Hubbard Dianetic Research Foundation in Wichita "to further pursue," in the words of the Foundation, "investigations into the incredible and fantastic." Hubbard ignored the jibe and immediately set up something which he called The Hubbard College. He had married once more—his new wife was a Texas girl named Mary Sue Whipp who had been active in the research foundation—and was busy developing the tenets of his new science: Scientology, an exact definition of which would be "Knowing how to know."

Scientology introduced theories and techniques which made the engrams and reveries of Dianetics look like a mild dress rehearsal. I will go into their absolutely monumental proportions later, but for the moment, to suggest a little something of what Hubbard was about, listen to this from one of the new books, *Scientology: The Fundamentals of Thought*. "Probably the greatest discovery of Scientology," Hubbard wrote, "and its most forceful contribution to the knowledge of mankind has been the isolation, description and handling of the human spirit. Accomplished in July, 1951, in Phoenix, Arizona, I established along scientific rather than religious or humanitarian lines that that thing which is the person, the personality, is separable from the body and the mind at will without causing bodily death or mental derangement." He named this "thing" the *theta*, after the Greek letter $\theta$, and said it possessed the capacity to create. What it created Hubbard called MEST, that acronym of the first letters of matter, energy, space, and time, the stuff of existence as we know it. Hubbard taught these theories and the techniques necessary to achieve a state of enlightened discovery of one's own *theta*. This became his new definition for *clear*, replacing the old dianetic notion, which now became the preliminary state to *clear*, and made of the person studying Scientology a *preclear*.

Hubbard taught all this at his Hubbard College, awarding graduates a degree of "Registered Dianeticist," with a license to give courses in dianetic processing in their own offices and schools. The cost of the course, which, when concluded, provided not only the degree but necessary films and texts, was originally $1,000. By March 1, 1952, the price had gone up to $1,500, and a few weeks later, on the twentieth, it went up to $2,000. On June 1, Hubbard raised it once more, to a flat $5,000.* At much the same time, he organized another corporation in Kansas, Scientific Press, Inc., which published and distributed the writings and texts used by his students and his "Registered Dianeticists." He also went to Phoenix, Arizona, and organized the Hubbard Association of Scientologists (HAS), stating that its purpose was to publish material related to behavior studies and to train qualified people in Scientology.

In early 1953 Hubbard went to Philadelphia and incorporated the Hubbard Association of Scientologists of Pennsylvania, Inc., and in the fall, opened HAS branches in Camden, New Jersey, and London, England. Things did not go well for Scientology either in Camden or Philadelphia, so early in 1954 he closed down both those operations and returned to Phoenix, now his headquarters, and incorporated the Hubbard Association of Scientologists International (HASI), Inc., presumably to facilitate Scientology's overseas expansion. He began publishing a periodical, *Scientology*, and offered a "Summary Course In Dianetics & Scientology" for $382.50.

---

* Records give no indication of how many people actually signed up for any of these courses, no matter what the cost.

He also set up a Hubbard College Graduate School and charged a flat $25 registration fee, offering a degree of Bachelor of Scientology. Electropsychometers, now called E-Meters, were also on sale, for $98.50. They had by this time completely replaced *dianetic reverie* and were essential to Scientology. Hubbard's brochures for the machines described them as capable of registering "relative degrees of dynamic psychophysical stress from moment to moment during the dianetic session," indicating "the approximate Hubbardian tone-scale of the preclear from 1.0 to *infinitely high ranges* [italics his]." He fixed the importance of the E-Meter once and for all when he wrote, in a later brochure: "Bluntly, auditing can't be at optimum without an electropsychometer. An auditor auditing without a machine reminds one of a hunter hunting ducks at pitch black midnight, firing his gun off in all directions."

By 1955, Dianetics had rejoined Hubbard's fold on something of an official basis. The Research Foundation in Los Angeles with whom he had broken had fallen on hard times and Hubbard was able to make some kind of peace with its directors. Hubbard celebrated this reunion by holding what he called a Unification Congress. But he was not about to throw his weight behind the reintroduction of the name "Dianetics." Scientology was doing well and it would have been foolish to drop it. In his own special way, Hubbard himself explained the reason for retaining "Scientology." In an article entitled "Scientology: A New Science," which was published in *Scientology* magazine in 1954, he wrote: "The basic science was named 'Scientology' in 1938. In 1947 L. Ron Hubbard [many of Scientology's articles, written in a style and syntax that can only be his, seek some special pertinence by being both anonymous and referring to Hubbard in the third person] changed its name to 'Dianetics' in order to make a social test of publication and popularity. The test completed, in 1952 he changed the science back to its original name,

Scientology. This was done to inhibit its being monopolized for private purposes." *

In June of 1955, Hubbard and his wife, Mary Sue, moved the center of his activities to Washington, D.C., where they set up The Founding Church of Scientology. That same year, in November, a Founding Church of Scientology was incorporated in New York as an unincorporated independent church "pursuant to Article 8 of the Religious Corporations Law," which states that "an 'unincorporated church' is a congregation, society, or other assemblage of persons who are accustomed to statedly meet for divine worship or other religious observances, without having been incorporated for that purpose." Scientology was able to qualify easily, and auditors and officers of The Founding Church of Scientology legitimately began to call themselves "ministers," defined by the same law as follows: "The term 'clergyman' and the term 'minister' include a duly authorized pastor, rector, priest, rabbi, and a person having authority from, or in accordance with, the rules and regulations of the governing ecclesiastical body of the denomination or order, if any, to which the church belongs, or otherwise from the church or synagogue to preside over and direct the spiritual affairs of the church or synagogue."

Some years later, Hubbard was asked by an interviewer why he had turned Scientology into a religion. "To some," he answered, "this seems mere opportunism, to some it would seem that Scientology is simply making itself bulletproof in the eyes of the law, and to some it might appear that any association with religion is a reduction of the ethics and purposes of Scientology itself. . . . Why should Scientology ally

* For the record, the name Scientology was first used by a German social psychologist, Dr. A. Nordenholz, who in 1934 published a book entitled *Scientologie: Science of the Constitution & Usefulness of Knowledge/Knowing* (Ernest Reinhardt, Munich). Its contents and relevance to Scientology will be discussed in greater detail elsewhere.

itself with religion? There are many, many reasons. Amongst them is that a society accords to men of the church an access not given to others. Prisons, hospitals, and institutions . . . cannot do otherwise than welcome men of the church. . . ."

In answer to what must have obviously been inquiries regarding the ritualistic nature of Scientology, the Founding Church eventually published a book entitled *Ceremonies of The Founding Church of Scientology.* It described the basic church services practiced by Scientology and gave outlines for sample sermons, as well as the procedure for weddings, christenings, and funerals. Most of the ceremonies are traditional, one might even call them basic, with Scientological acknowledgments of aspects of mortality and immortality not unlike those expressed by other faiths. Only the christening ceremony stands out as somewhat unique, free to express itself more along the lines of Scientology's theology. The section for this ceremony explains that, "the main purpose of a Christening is to help get the thetan oriented. He has recently taken over his new body. He is aware that it is his and that he is operating it. However he has never been told the identity of his body."

As an example, an informal christening service Hubbard performed in 1957 is reprinted. Addressing himself to the babe, he introduced the parents and designated godparents to those gathered. Then, still addressing the child, he continued: "How are you? All right. Now your name is _____. You got that? Good. There you are. Did that upset you? Now, do you realize that you're a member of HASI? Pretty good, huh? All right. Now I want to introduce you to your father. This is Mr. _____. (To the parent): Come over here. (To the child): And here's your mother. And now, in case you get into trouble and want to borrow some quarters here's Mr. _____. See him? He's your godfather. Now, take a look at him. That's right. And here's _____, in case you want some real good auditing; she's your godmother. Got it? Now you are suitably christened. Don't worry about it, it could be worse. O.K. Thank you very much. They'll treat you all right."

For the years between 1955, when Hubbard came to Washington, D.C., and 1959, when he and Mary Sue left for England, The Founding Church of Scientology was the "Mother Church." All Scientology churches and congregations in the United States, as well as locally incorporated branches of either a local HASI or the Phoenix corporation, were under the leadership and guidance of L. Ron Hubbard. Advertisements for The Founding Church of Scientology in local newspapers made little reference to its activities as a religious organization. Their messages were directed more to the improvement of an individual's health, personality, and techniques to increase one's I.Q., as well as offering guidance in problems of marriage and the raising of children. In the Yellow Pages, Scientology was listed under three categories: "Personal Development," "Personal Consultants," and "Churches—Various Denominations."

The Founding Church of Scientology offered a three-week intensive processing course for $1,250, and practiced a variety of methods designed to increase the rolls of its membership. Among the most prominent in the late fifties were three Hubbard had outlined in issue No. 73 of the *Professional Auditors Bulletin*: "I Will Talk To Anyone," "Illness Researches," and "Casualty Contact." The first involved the placing of newspaper advertisements which announced: "Personal counseling—I will talk to anyone for you about anything. Phone Reverend so-and-so between hour and hour." When someone would call the reverend and try to explain a particular problem, he would explain, with utmost discretion, that it was impossible to discuss a case over the telephone and please to come in personally. "Illness Researches" also involved the placing of advertisements in newspapers, but these read: "Polio Victims. A research foundation, investigating polio, desires volunteers suffering from the after effects of that

illness to call for examination at _____." Anyone coming in
would find himself being audited and then strongly urged to
join The Founding Church of Scientology.

Typically, Hubbard justified any suggestion of duplicity by
writing, "It was given under the guise of investigation and
was in actuality a research project. . . . Any auditor can con-
stitute himself as a minister or an auditor, a research worker
in the field of any illness. In that he is not offering to treat or
cure the illness but is strictly investigating it, the laws concerning medicine do not obtain to him. Anybody, even a
ditch-digger, can look over polio or arthritis or asthma or
anything else." Thus his instructions continued: "It is best that
a minister representing himself as a 'charitable organization,'
which is what he is, do the research so that the advertisement
would then read: 'Polio victims—a charitable organization
investigating polio desires to examine several victims of the
after effects of this illness. Phone so and so."

Grimmest of all the methods was "Casualty Contact," which
Hubbard calmly described as follows:

> One takes every daily paper he can get his hands on and cuts
> from it every story whereby he might have a preclear. He
> either has the address in the story itself or he gets the address
> as a minister from the newspaper. As speedily as possible he
> makes a call on the bereaved or injured person. . . . He should
> represent himself to the person or the person's family as a
> minister whose compassion was compelled by the newspaper
> story concerning the person. He should then enter the presence
> of the person and give a nominal assist, leave his card which
> states exactly where church services are held every Sunday
> and with the statement that a much fuller recovery is possible
> by coming to these free services takes his departure. A great
> many miracles will follow in his wake and he is later to become
> a subject of the press himself. However, in handling the press
> we should simply say that it is a mission of the Church to
> assist those who are in need of assistance.

Anticipating that certain practices and policies of his Founding Church of Scientology might run into trouble, Hubbard

organized something called the National Academy of American Psychology, and in 1957 sent out a "loyalty oath" to psychologists, psychiatrists, psychoanalysts, and "ministers of various denominations who engage in mental practice." The oath's text was reprinted in Scientology's *Certainty* magazine, in 1958, as follows:

> I hereby subscribe to the following Code of Ethics and Practice and swear to abide by it at all times.
>
> I do solemnly swear:
>
> 1) To support and defend the Constitution of the United States against all enemies, foreign and domestic; that I will bear true faith and allegiance to same.
>
> 2) To refuse to practice "Brainwashing" upon American citizens.
>
> 3) To actively prevent the teaching of only foreign psychology in public schools and universities.
>
> 4) To engage in no conspiracy to commit or "treat" persons for purely self-interested or political reasons.
>
> 5) To refuse to protect criminals by supporting questionable pleas of insanity at trials.
>
> 6) To discourage all violence against the mentally ill.
>
> 7) To refuse to use, advocate or experiment with physical methods of "therapy" upon patients which might bring about incapacitating physical injury to the patient's brain tissue or body.
>
> 8) To use only methods of mental practice or techniques of therapy upon patients which I would willingly experience myself to the same extent or duration that I apply them or advocate that they be applied.
>
> 9) To refuse to contribute money, dues or my services to organizations which knowingly impede American scientific research programs or which work to discredit American psychologists to the public.
>
> 10) To refute propaganda to the effect that the study of psychology is hopeless, that I.Q. cannot be improved and that personality cannot be changed.
>
> 11) To refuse to accept for counseling or psychological assistance and to refuse to accept money from any patient or group I feel I cannot honestly help and to offer no solution or cure I cannot accomplish.

12) To refuse to advertise beyond the display of my professional card and the supported claims of my school of mental practice.

13) To render good treatment, sound training and good discipline to those students or people entrusted to my care.

14) To engage in no unseemly disputes with the uninformed on the subject of my profession.

15) To refuse to interfere with the lives of my patients beyond actual treatment.

16) To refer to competent medical treatment, ills which demand medical attention.

17) To hold in confidence the secrets of my patients.

18) To accept as fellow psychologists only psychologists adhering to this code and to speak no words of criticism in public of them.

I take this obligation freely, without any mental reservations, or purpose of evasion: So help me God.

Hubbard wrapped up his ingenious, all-purpose loyalty oath by announcing that anyone who refused to sign it—it was not only to be signed, with two witnesses, but "subscribed and sworn to before" a notary public—would be classified "potentially subversive," while anyone who dared to "rail" against it would be openly branded "subversive" and his name would be turned over to the Federal government for "appropriate action."

Over the years Hubbard's running war with psychiatry and psychology has, if anything, become more ferocious. Last spring, he wrote: "The psychiatrist and his front groups operate straight out of the terrorist text books. The Mafia looks like a convention of Sunday School teachers compared to these terrorist groups."

I could never make out a consistent pattern to Hubbard's restless and continual establishment of new organizations designed to advance and disseminate the world of Scientology. They seem more motivated by an urge to keep things *moving*, generating a kind of business which implies importance. There is something of the overworked, hyper-pressured conglomerate executive in the way Hubbard threw together—legally incorporating every time—groups, organizations, and associations. All of it had that smell of the grandiose but insubstantial, the quickie letterhead house designed to keep you from asking too many "technical" questions. Rather than allow Hubbard's various ventures to confound me, I carefully took them apart, one by one, tried to describe their function, and then located the links which represented his ever-expanding network. It all leads to no small appreciation of the shining versatility he had for generating Scientological activities, *all* of which he controlled absolutely.

In 1955, Hubbard incorporated something called the Congress of Eastern Scientologists, a name which, in 1957, he changed for some obscure business reason to the Congress of Scientologists. During the four years of his Washington, D.C., activities, two congresses were held, each lasting a few days, normally two, at a hotel in the city. In 1956, some 450 people attended "The Games Congress," and in 1958 about 140 persons paid $800 each to attend a second congress. Hubbard personally made all the plans and worked out each program for the conventions. He wrote and delivered all the lectures, and for all this he was paid a fee by the Congress of Scientologists, Inc., a total of $22,683.94 for his energetic contribution and participation on the two occasions.

Hubbard incorporated a Washington, D.C., branch of HASI in 1957, and until 1959 its operations were directed by a three-member board of directors, two of whom were Hubbard and his wife, Mary Sue. Between them they had the power to elect all officers. In addition to being on the board of directors of The Founding Church of Scientology as well as working on and being personally responsible for every facet of Scientology's activities, Hubbard was also the organization's financial manager and had complete operational responsibility for all fiscal affairs. This control encompassed not only HASI and The Founding Church of Scientology, but yet another organization called the Distribution Center, Inc., which was responsible for the printing and distribution of all Scientology publications. The business of books had become particularly important to Hubbard because, as he put it, they made "thousands in money and friends" for Scientology. A new book appeared on an average of one every six months and resulted in local sales of between 6,000 and 9,000 copies, recovering all printing costs in approximately eighty days.

Quite simply, Hubbard ran Scientology like a very tight ship. A disbursement sheet of each week's financial activities had to be on his desk by 2 P.M. of the Monday of the following week. He personally hired and fired each and every member of the staff. He supervised all processing and read all of the auditor's reports. He wrote the teaching materials for the elementary course then being taught, the Personal Efficiency Course, and he also taught it. All awards of certificates were made by him personally. And in his office safe he had signed resignations from every officer and trustee of every Scientology church in the country.

Until 1959, everyone in Scientology worked on straight salary. Then Hubbard made a few changes. He created a new post, HCO Accounts, HCO standing for the Hubbard Communications Office, and he appointed Mary Sue director of accounts. From then on she received weekly income sheets showing the total income from HASI, Inc., and DCI, Inc. At the same time, Hubbard stopped paying straight salaries and introduced a percentage or commission system of payment. Hubbard himself was paid 10 percent of all gross income. Outside Washington, D.C., Scientology churches and organizations paid this amount into a local HCO account.

Anyone owing Scientology money became the subject of a collection folder. Each folder had copies of any outstanding invoices and a careful record of all payments made. In addition, folders contained copies of all contracts and due notes—people were allowed in effect to borrow money from Scientology to pay for being in Scientology. Once a month, these folders were summarized and statements were sent out. If somebody was late to pay, The Founding Church often mailed out collection letters, some of them rather harshly worded and not averse to threatening legal action. Past-due notes were also turned over to collection agencies.

In March of 1959, Hubbard and Mary Sue left Washington, D.C., and moved to England, where Scientology was already well established. Rather than settle in London, Hubbard chose Saint Hill Manor, a splendid English mansion which had been built in 1728, located just outside the small town of East Grinsted, in Sussex, some thirty miles from London. The Manor had at one time been the property of Mrs. Anthony Drexel Biddle, who had sold it to the Maharaja of Jaipur. In 1959 it became Scientology's world headquarters, presided over with baronial reserve by L. Ron Hubbard, who soon acquired a chauffeur, a car to be driven in, a Jaguar for himself, and a staff headed by a butler named Shepheardson who every afternoon brought Hubbard a bottle of Coca-Cola on a silver tray.

Through the extensive deployment of a Telex network on behalf of HCO (WW)—Hubbard Communications Office, World-Wide—Hubbard maintained split-second communication with all of the HASI and Scientology Church organizations throughout the world. While he was actively involved in the day-to-day operation of these various HASI and church branches, it was via HCO (WW) that he produced the never-ending stream of bulletins, policy letters and information letters. These communiqués were crucial because they spelled out, in no uncertain terms, *exactly* what the latest technique was, or how official policy had been changed. They were identifiable not only by name, but by color of ink as well. HCO Bulletins were normally printed in bright red ink, with a headline at the top announcing the procedure to be discussed. HCO Policy Letters were printed in green ink and would discuss anything from a specific policy change to a general warning about "Things That Shouldn't Be." HCO Information Letters came in blue ink and tended to be rather chatty. Each type of letter bore a legend explaining to whom distribution was to be made, as for example: "Remimeo: All Students, All Staff." Conversely, any communiqués from people in the field were sent directly to HCO (WW), though protocol dictated the notion that they were addressing themselves to HASI, Ltd. Hubbard himself described the proper function of HCO (WW) in an HCO information letter dated February 18, 1964. "HCO (WW) Ltd.," he wrote, "is concerned with the Organizations of Scientology on a world wide basis. It deals with Ron's personal communications to and from the HCO's, ORGS and Field, and with the Franchise Holders. It sends out Ron's policies and technical data. It has its own direct line to the HCO's, ORGS and City Offices all over the world." In addition, though not necessarily through HCO (WW), a weekly report on the processing of every *preclear* throughout the world was forwarded to Hubbard at Saint Hill.

In the years that followed Hubbard's arrival at Saint Hill, there was both a mellowing and a refinement in his policies for bringing new people into Scientology. The somewhat grisly methods of "Illness Researches" and "Casualty Contact" seem to have been forsaken for a more direct, snappy, businesslike approach. In an HCO Bulletin of April 9, 1960, Hubbard wrote:

> When the prospect comes in, see him or her at once (No waiting). Be courteous, friendly, businesslike. Rise when they enter and leave. Call reception to show them out if they stay too long. Be willing to take their money. Always prefer cash to notes. We are not a credit company. Always see the student or the pc [preclear] before they leave the place after service. You can often sell more training or processing. . . . It is a maxim that unless you have bodies in the shop you get no

income. So on any pretext get the bodies in the place and provide ingress to the Registrar when they're there.

By 1965, through obvious trial and error, Hubbard was outlining the only way a local organization should set up its courses and services. Writing in an HCO Policy Letter dated August 13, 1965, he said:

> One must NEVER recruit a body of people and then carry just that group up, opening new courses only when they are ready and closing the lower ones when emptied. I can tell you by grim experience that that is NOT the way to handle basic courses. . . . One must continually nightly recruit new people and one must have in existence the next area up for them to move into. . . . The assembly line must exist before one can get traffic to put on it. . . . The key is standardize. Even out the traffic flow.

Hubbard went on to describe the proper allotment of space for the courses being given. He was emphatic on the need for an organization to have a separate reception room.

> If you don't have a public reception centre and only have your org Comm Centre you ought to be ashamed and no wonder your receptionist and comm lines jam up. Public Reception ought to be separate. It should be plastered with promotion, personality graphs, tone scales, anything promotional. And the evening Introductory Lecture is given *every* evening. Same lecture.

Hubbard went on to urge heavy advertising of the free introductory lecture. He also urged each organization to "Get a Chaplain on the job and prominently display this sign: If you are in trouble with your training or Processing and nobody seems to listen, see the Chaplain, Room _____. He can help." Then, Hubbard explained, "groove in the Chaplain to be a Problems Officer, to listen and try to straighten up goofs by auditors and supervisors and suddenly your student and pc loss rate will almost vanish." Finally, Hubbard urged everyone to "Be Good. Your courses now *have* to be good. Your income depends not on enrollment but reenrollment . . . be crisp."

A proper, steady flow of new people into Scientology was particularly important to Hubbard, at Saint Hill, because the local churches and organizations throughout the world could take fledgling scientologists only up to a certain stage. Beyond that, actually to approach and then realize the pure state of "clear," they all had to make the trip to England, at their own expense, of course, and take their advanced grades of release; for the truly ultra-dedicated there was also another course, the Saint Hill Special Briefing Course. Quite obviously, if the source of new Scientologists was improperly managed, the number of people, considering a normal statistical attrition or percentage of dropouts, who would ultimately make that pilgrimage to Saint Hill, would simply dwindle.

In 1963 Scientology faced its first major challenge when the United States government filed suit requesting "seizure and condemnation of a certain article of device, hereinafter set forth," in accordance with laws established and enforced by the Food and Drug Administration. What the FDA was talking about was the E-Meter, and a complaint was filed on January 4, 1963. A lawful writ was issued and in short order the Founding Church of Scientology in Washington, D.C., was raided. E-Meters and books were seized, and further charges were filed.

Hubbard knew the FDA had been nosing around his activities and tried to promulgate a change in the use of the E-Meter by Scientology. In an HCO Policy Letter dated October 29, 1962, he wrote that "regardless of any earlier uses of psychogalvanometers in Dianetics or Psychology or in early Scientology publications when research was in progress, the Electrometer in Scientology today has *no* other use" except to "disclose truth to the individual who is being processed and thus free him spiritually." The E-Meter, he went on, "is a valid religious instrument, used in Confessionals, and is in no way diagnostic and does not treat."

This declaration did not seem to help Scientology's predicament. The meters were seized, and the government charged that

> in that the labeling for the E-Meter contains statements which represent, suggest and imply that the E-Meter is adequate and effective for diagnosis, prevention, treatment, detection and elimination of the causes of all mental and nervous disorders and illnesses such as neuroses, psychoses, schizophrenia, and all psychosomatic ailments of mankind such as arthritis, cancer, stomach ulcers, and radiation burns from atomic bombs, poliomyelitis, the common cold, etc., and that the article is adequate and effective to improve the intelligence quotient, and to measure the basal metabolism, mental state and change of state of man; which statements are false and misleading. . . .

Scientology appealed, arguing that the search and seizure had been illegal, but some months later, from Saint Hill, Hubbard, something of a pillar of calm, issued an HCO Bulletin which said, "Government attacks have entered a more desultory stage. Meters will go to jury trial eventually and we will certainly win. The U.S. Government Attorney handling the case became terribly ill and had to resign it."

Hubbard was wrong and Scientology lost its appeal that the case be thrown out of court. The case was finally heard, and on April 19, 1967, more than four years having gone by, a decision was returned against Scientology, directing that the meters and all accompanying literature be destroyed. Scientology immediately appealed, again claiming illegal search and seizure. At the same time, Scientology's lawyers deposited a brief which suggested that all E-Meters be labeled as follows: "The Hubbard Electrometer is not intended for use in or effective for the diagnosis, cure, mitigation, treatment or prevention of any disease." It was their hope that this disclaimer would satisfy the FDA and inspire withdrawal of the destroy order. Though the government did not accept the proposals, all meters still in use were subsequently labeled with a message which reads: "The E-Meter is not intended or effective for the diagnosis, treatment or prevention of any disease."

In February of 1969, the U.S. Court of Appeals in Washington, D.C., handed down its decision on Scientology's appeal. It reversed the decision of the federal jury and stated that until the government can offer proof that Scientology is not a religion, the E-Meters and the literature seized are protected by our rights of freedom of worship. The decision, which was handed down by Judge J. Skelly Wright, said that from the point of view of Scientology, "auditing or processing is a central practice of their religion, akin to confession in the Catholic Church." Since the E-Meters do state that they are not used to diagnose or treat physical ills, but merely to work on the spirit, all accompanying E-Meter literature must be treated as Scripture.

Possibly because of the FDA's publicized interest and activities in 1963, Australia's Scientologists found themselves, that same year, the object of much scrutiny and criticism. By November of the year outcries reached such proportions that a formal board of inquiry, in the person of Queens Counselor Kevin Victor Anderson, was named.

Scientology had arrived in Australia in 1956. During the years which followed, it had become strongly established, particularly in Melbourne, in the state of Victoria. From the very beginning, Scientology's activities had drawn some curiosity on the part of civil authorities, but it was not until the press began to attack it publicly that demands were made in the Legislative Council that something be done. The Board of Inquiry was the result.

Hubbard had visited Australia in 1959 and, enthusiastic about the success his branches were enjoying, advanced the notion that Australia would be the world's first totally *clear* continent. Based on something he called his "Special Zone

Plan," he devised a plan through which he intended to bring the Australian Labor Party into Scientology. In January of 1961 he wrote Peter Roger Williams, Scientology's continental director for Australia, New Zealand, and Oceania:

> My goals for the Zone Plan are to make my organization a Scientology Organization with all executives HPA (Hubbard Professional Auditor) graduates, and to use our publications to improve administration, management and communication in the Labor movement and interest the Australian Labor Party and Trade Union officials in taking scientology training. The Australian Labor Party as an organization using scientology principles would soon win a Government as soon as the next Federal election. With Australia led by a government employing scientology principles we should soon have a civilization which can extend influence overseas.*

In the beginning, Australian Scientologists welcomed the Board of Inquiry enthusiastically and proclaimed that the findings would once and for all vindicate Scientology and Dianetics. Hubbard himself went even further and said that the Board had actually been appointed because of Scientology's insistence that such an official investigation be made. The Melbourne HASI offices cooperated fully and made their records available to the Board. Demonstration sessions were organized, both in auditing and exercises, and facilities were provided for the playing of Hubbard's taped lectures. Hub-

---

* The notion of scientology using its principles to improve management is not at all far-fetched and has become something of a reality. Several management consultant firms based on Scientology are active in the United States. For two years now, a successful scientologist named Alan Walter has been working with executives at the home office of Tenneco Oil Company, Dallas, Texas. Another management course is being taught in Austin, Texas, by a man named John McCoy. McCoy has also made a proposal to the administrator of the entire public school system of the state of Florida and it is claimed that a program is being developed by which all Florida public school teachers will be instructed in Scientology techniques to achieve more effectiveness in their classrooms. Furthermore, General Electric's Information Systems Department in Bethesda, Maryland, is said to be considering a management proposal made by Scientology Consultants to Management, a firm operated by Paul and Gloria Nickel.

bard himself was invited to appear before the Board, but declined. Then, in October of 1964, Hubbard's lawyers requested that the state of Victoria pay his way from England to fly to Australia to give evidence. The request was refused, and the Board concluded that Hubbard had no intention of ever making such a trip; knowing his request would be rejected, he was using the rejection to criticize the conduct of the Board and its subsequent findings. All enthusiasm was gone and no more cooperation was given. Any notions of a Scientological Australia had been dashed in May of 1964, prior to the 1964 Victorian elections, when Williams, Scientology's continental director, had written an article in the Melbourne HASI Communications Magazine entitled "A Declaration of War." "It is the urgent duty of every scientologist in Victoria," he wrote, "to get out and make certain that the Australian Labor Party is defeated completely and thoroughly and forever at the election." His hostility, Williams explained later, was not political but stemmed from the ALP's wholly negative attitude towards HASI.

The final sitting of the Board of Inquiry was held on April 21, 1965, and a report was submitted on September 28, 1965. The Board had sat in hearing for 160 days, heard 151 witnesses, filed 621 numbered exhibits, and took 8,920 pages of testimony. To the best of its ability, it examined Scientology, as well as its predecessor, Dianetics, from every conceivable angle: the theories, the teaching of Scientology, its relationship to religion, the E-Meter, its healing claims, the financial aspects, the alleged benefits of Scientology processing, and the processes themselves. While there is, in the published report, a tendency towards repetition, as well as a fairly clear expression of one man's attitude as influenced by his personal spiritual beliefs, there is also, despite an avowed determination to remain objective, an overall failure fully to grasp either the source or intention of Hubbard's theories, as well as the ramification of the processes, techniques and exercises which go beyond even the many case histories studied and discussed. Yet one conclusion is stated in no uncertain terms: "However Hubbard may appear to his devoted followers, the Board can form no other view than that Hubbard is a fraud and scientology fraudulent."

On December 4, 1965, the state of Victoria passed an act "to provide for the Registration of Psychologists, the Protection of the Public from Unqualified Persons and certain Harmful Practices and for other purposes." It was a sweeping measure, only a part of which—Part III: "Hypnotism and other practices"—dealt directly with Scientology. Use of the E-Meter by anyone other than a registered psychologist or someone who has received the consent of the Council became punishable by a fine of A$500. The teaching and/or application of Scientology was to be fined A$200 for the first offense, and A$500 plus a prison term of not more than two years for a second offense. Scientology was specifically defined as being the teachings and writings of L. Ron Hubbard as disseminated by HASI. The law further directed that any and all "scientological records" be delivered to the Attorney General. Failure to do so was liable to a fine of not more than A$200. Upon passage of the bill the police moved swiftly and raided the Melbourne HASI headquarters, seizing some 4,000 personal files.

Hubbard's answer was immediate. He issued a booklet entitled "Kangaroo Court," in which he referred to the transport in the 1700's of convicts from England to the state of Victoria. "The foundation of Victoria," he wrote, "consists of the riff-raff of London's slums, robbers, murderers, prostitutes, fences, thieves. . . . The insane attack on Scientology can best be understood if Victoria is seen for what it is—a very primitive community, somewhat barbaric, with a rudimentary knowledge of the physical sciences. In fact, it is a scientific barbarism so bigoted that they know not and do not know they are ignorant."

Victoria's neighboring state of New South Wales, possibly

because of the very negative reaction to the speedy seizure of Scientology papers and records, and in light of a declaration that there had been no significant increase in mental hospital admissions which could be directly attributed to Scientology, decided at the time of the Victorian passage of the law to take no action. The feeling was expressed in some N.S.W. government circles that passing a similar law would be like "using a sledgehammer to crack a walnut." At the same time, the obviously relieved secretary and director of Scientology's N.S.W. headquarters eagerly invited reporters to come in and see Scientology for themselves. They wanted to give "the public a little more information than they already have," and went on to explain that they "do not in any way at all, deal in the realms of psychology, psychiatry, healing, hypnotism or any of the other things we are accused of stating that we are authorities on." In 1966, the New South Wales Minister of Health, answering a question in the Legislative Assembly, said "we have come to the conclusion that there is little or no evidence that action should be taken to ban the organization in New South Wales." *

As if the turmoil of both the Victorian ban and the FDA

---

* The question of whether or not to ban Scientology in N.S.W. was raised again in 1968. Western Australia was introducing a bill to ban Scientology, South Australia had already passed one. But the Minister for Health for N.S.W., Mr. A. H. Jago, said that in N.S.W. "there is very little incidence of the more unfavourable features of this organisation." Thus, once again, N.S.W. did not act against the movement. Later the same month, the British-based headquarters of Scientology announced that they were making a A$2,679,000 interest-free loan to Scientology in Victoria, where it had been banned since 1965. The announcement said that the money would be used to build a "new study centre for art, culture, and humanity." The Sydney Morning Herald reported the loan and said that "local businessmen and civic leaders, with a record of honesty and integrity, would be invited to serve as trustees, a spokesman at the headquarters, near London, said." The story went on to say that Victoria's Minister for Health, Mr. V. O. Dickie, was doubtful that any Melbourne business or civic leaders would "have a bar of it. We have," he was quoted as saying, "an act which outlaws the teaching of scientology in this State, but we shall have to wait and see just what their real intentions are with this proposed study centre."

case was not enough, by 1966 the Internal Revenue Service in this country was taking a very hard look at The Founding Church of Scientology, its structure, and its activities over the years since its incorporation. Hubbard, in England, possibly worn out by all the hassling, or simply exercising his prodigious talent for anticipation, made a dramatic move and publicly announced he was leaving Scientology forever. He sold his interests in HASI, Ltd., for 100,000 pounds sterling—$280,000 at the time—relinquishing the organization's "goodwill," as well as any legal responsibilities, and, in a move which stunned everyone, left for Rhodesia, where he reportedly bought a house on Lake Kariba and appeared on local television to repeat that he had finished with Scientology. His English followers, beset by all kinds of rumors, were immensely relieved when his self-imposed exile was briskly terminated, some say by the Rhodesian government, and he returned to England. His followers' concern may have been due to the fact that in 1964 Hubbard had stated that he had been approached by Fidel Castro's official representatives interested in sending a picked group of fifty to Saint Hill for Scientology training. Hubbard went on to say that as early as 1938 the Soviet Union was courting his services. "I was put under considerable argument and stress," he had told a reporter in 1964. "They offered me $200,000, all laboratory facilities, everything I needed in Russia." His answer was No, he said, adding that as a result his apartment "was blasted open," and his "basic manuscript"—he may have been referring to *Excalibur*—disappeared.

Once back in England Hubbard did not stay long, and soon retreated to the Mediterranean, where he ensconced himself as the commodore of the Scientological fleet, that he named his *Sea Org*, plying the warm waters of the Levant with a full crew of dedicated Scientologists on board, developing new techniques and making even newer discoveries. The Hubbard flagship is an old passenger ferry and ex-cattle boat, originally christened the *Royal Scotsman*. There is also a former Hull trawler, the *Avonriver*, and a yacht, *Enchanter*. More recently, when the *Sea Org* was made to feel unwelcome in Spanish ports, Hubbard made for the Greek Isles and chose Corfu as a land-base of operations. To please the Greek government, the ships were renamed *Apollo*, *Athena*, and *Diana*. I heard some vague reports that soon after Hubbard's arrival, the American consul in Corfu began receiving requests from scientologists aboard the ships asking for help to get off. This seems somewhat substantiated by the reports, in March 1969, that the Greek government suddenly gave Hubbard and about two hundred of the disciples twenty-four hours to get out—cast off from their Corfu moorings, actually. According to *The New York Times*, "the expulsion order followed months of pressure in Athens by American, British and Australian diplomats urging Greek authorities to examine the activities of the *Apollo* residents, most of them . . . Americans, but some . . . from Britain, Australia and South Africa." Whether the Greek government went to the trouble of examining these activities is open to question. What they did was brand the crowd "undesirables" and told them to get out. At the moment, I do not know where, exactly, the winds of chance have carried Hubbard's defiant little fleet. I do know that it has expanded to include seven vessels with names such as *Apollo*, *Athena*, *Diana*, *Neptune*, and *Aries*. The *Athena* is currently anchored off the coast of Denmark, while *Neptune* is supposedly assigned to the Pacific Flotilla which I take to be the two Sea Org ships anchored off Santa Monica, California.

Hubbard's role with regard to Scientology is virtually intact. He is still director of HCO (WW), collecting his 10 percent as paid in to HCO (WW). (With an estimated weekly gross income of $1.4 million, this means Hubbard is taking in $140,-000 a week.) He keeps in constant touch with Scientology centers all over the world by way of his direct communications link to HASI, Ltd., at Saint Hill and the American Saint Hill

Organization in Los Angeles. His hold had been additionally strengthened by the fact that his faithful wife, Mary Sue, bore until recently the official designation of "Guardian W.W.," a post now held by a Scientologist named Jane Kember.

Hubbard's departure from England in no way affected the IRS inquiries. Contending that The Founding Church of Scientology had a substantial nonreligious and commercial aspect to it through the sale of processing and training services, books, pamphlets, and E-Meters, the argument was simply that Scientology had not operated "exclusively" for religious and educational purposes, as defined in section 501 (c)(3) of the Internal Revenue Code of 1954. It was discovered that during the four years, from 1956 to June of 1959, that Hubbard and his wife, Mary Sue, operated The Founding Church of Scientology in Washington, D.C., the organization took in gross receipts totaling $758,962 in Washington alone, and that during those four years never less than 90 percent of this gross income came from processing and training, rather than from something as clearly religious in nature as donations.

The government argued that Scientology's intentions and practice was to make money and to charge substantial sums for its services and to sell the books, not give them away. This was backed by citing Hubbard's HCO Policy Letter of January 30, 1966: "Money is a symbol. It represents success when you have it, and defeat when you don't, no matter who is putting out propaganda to the contrary."

The government also discovered that from the time Hubbard had left Washington for Saint Hill, the weekly 10 percent paid him by all affiliated Scientology churches and organizations and franchised branches was going directly to him in the name of HCO (WW). Some of the checks, the government found, had been desposited directly into Swiss banks.

The case was finally argued in July of 1967. Even before an opinion was handed down, Scientology churches in other states were in trouble. The California church, which had been granted tax exemption on January 2, 1957, found itself served on January 6, 1967, with a proposed revocation of that status effective back to January 1957. The same thing happened to the churches in New York, Michigan, and Florida. All faced the possibility of being hit for back taxes for periods as long as ten years.

In August of 1968, an "opinion" of a trial commissioner of the Court of Claims was affirmed. It favored revocation of the tax-exempt status of The Founding Church of Scientology in Washington, the Mother Church. The decision was immediately appealed. One year later, in the summer of 1969, the full court heard the appeal and held against The Founding Church of Scientology. This opened the road for the Internal Revenue Service to move not only against the Washington Church, but also the other Scientology churches throughout the country. No one can say exactly how much Scientology will be made to pay in back taxes. In the case of The Founding Church of Scientology in Washington, the IRS will be figuring from 1956, with 6 percent interest. Spread that through the country, and it must be the kind of penalty monies capable of hitting Scientology a very serious, if not crippling blow.

There are few legal maneuvers left open to Scientology. After losing the appeal in Washington, the church moved for a rehearing, asking the court to be good enough to look at what they did all over again. If that fails, they will certainly go to the Supreme Court and ask for a review of the case. My personal opinion is that it will be extremely difficult for The Founding Church of Scientology to have its case reviewed because the weight of the Court of Claims decision in the summer of 1969 rested on the enormous sums of money L. Ron Hubbard and his family have taken out of Scientology's operation. What was demonstrated to the satisfaction of that court was not that Scientology was functioning as something other than an organization with spiritual overtones, but that it was functioning for the profit of somebody, that somebody being L. Ron Hubbard.

The British government, during the summer of 1968 when Scientology lost the first round of its tax case in Washington, was forced to respond to growing concern on the part of some English citizens and to sharp questions being asked in the House of Commons. It clamped a restriction on non-English nationals from entering the country solely for the purpose of studying or practicing Scientology. England's experience with Scientology was more direct and tumultuous than elsewhere because Hubbard had, until 1966, made Saint Hill Scientology's world headquarters and shrine.

As early as 1960, Hubbard was wildly sniping away at English critics. Taking on the British Medical Association, he wrote, in an HCO Bulletin, July 24, 1960: "With what amazed surprise we viewed the recent attack upon us by the British Medical Association. With their hands caked with blood they sought to point a grisly finger at us and to bring down upon us the wrath of the government they claimed they controlled. Folly, thy name is medicine. . . . I have found that the British Medical Association in England . . . has encouraged its doctors to spread vicious lies about us via their patients."

Although the English have a traditional tolerance for all kinds of legally expressed invective, it was inevitable that the matter of Scientology would find its way to the House of Commons. In February of 1966, the Minister of Health, Mr. Kenneth Robinson, answered some very general questions put to him regarding Scientology. In March of 1967 the debate resumed, this time much more heatedly. Peter Hordern, Conservative M.P. from Horsham, rose to bring to the attention of the House the case of one of his constituents, an emotionally disturbed young girl who became associated with Scientology only to end up under medical supervision. Hordern related the findings of the Board of Inquiry in Australia and ended by requesting that a full inquiry be made in the United Kingdom.

In response the Minister of Health acknowledged his personal concern with the question, then discussed "whether the scientologists in England carry out the same practices as did their counterparts in Australia and, if so, whether we should take the same view of them as did the state of Victoria?"

"This leads to the crucial question: to what can we reasonably take objection in Scientology," he continued. "For a Minister of Health, the overriding consideration must be the effect of these practices on mental health. Here, one must distinguish between what the leaders of the cult currently claim and what they have until recently professed and, in my judgment, still perform."

Mr. Robinson went on to consider whether or not Scientology attempts to heal, citing a letter Hubbard had written the Minister of Health disclaiming any such practices. Pointing out that there is nothing illegal occurring when unskilled people offer techniques through which they intend to relieve or remove mental troubles, because no claims for medical skills are made, he stated that there was no need for an inquiry because it was quite clear to him that Scientology was potentially harmful. Yet he closed by saying he hesitated to suggest that Scientology be prohibited. "My present view," he stated, "is that this would not be the right course to take, and I say this for several reasons. Legislation would certainly be necessary to achieve prohibition because, as I have said, medically unqualified people are within the law in offering or providing treatment with certain very limited exceptions. We would all, I believe, be reluctant to contemplate legislation—which would, on the Victoria pattern, almost inevitably have to range considerably beyond its immediate object if it were to be effective—unless the case for it were overwhelming. We are not in that position—at any rate, not yet."

East Grinsted, whose inhabitants their M.P. had said were seriously disturbed by Scientology, had been the center of all the unrest. With Saint Hill Manor just over the hill, the people of the village found themselves inundated with growing numbers of scientologists from all over the world, particularly from the United States and Australia. It was not long before HASI, Ltd., bought a hotel and many private houses and began to buy up and run some of the private businesses. Hubbard was a director of two local companies and his wife, Mary Sue, was a director of five, one with a reported nominal capital of £300,000 sterling. Early in June of 1968, in retaliation for criticism in the town, Saint Hill issued a proclamation that twenty-two of the town's businesses, including the local pub, the Rose & Crown, were off limits.

Finally, on July 25, 1968, in Written Answers in the House of Commons, Health Minister Robinson announced that certain actions would be taken with regard to Scientology:

> a) The Hubbard College of Scientology and all other scientology establishments, will no longer be accepted as educational establishments for the purposes of Home Office policy on the admission and subsequent control of foreign nationals;
> b) Foreign nationals arriving at United Kingdom ports who intend to proceed to scientology establishments will no longer be eligible for admission as students;
> c) Foreign nationals who are already in the United Kingdom, for example as visitors, will not be granted student status for the purpose of attending a scientology establishment;
> d) Foreign nationals already in the United Kingdom for study at a scientology establishment will not be granted extensions of stay to continue these studies;
> e) Work permits and employment vouchers will not be issued to foreign nationalists (or Commonwealth citizens) for work at a scientology establishment;
> f) Work permits already issued to foreign nationals for work at a scientology establishment will not be extended.

In August, the Home Office barred 800 Scientologists from entering England to attend a Scientology congress. In October, Mr. Alexander Lyons, M.P. from York, asked the Home Secretary how many persons had been denied entry into England because they were Scientologists. Mr. Lyon wanted to know

under what powers the immigration officers had acted if entry
had been refused. Mr. Callaghan, in written reply, said that
no one had been refused admission on the sole ground that
"he was a scientologist; but since July 25, 104 foreign nationals
intending to study at Scientology establishments have been
refused leave to land under the Aliens order, 1953." It was
clear that despite continuing apprehension regarding Scientology and its activities at Saint Hill, members of Parliament
were equally concerned about actions which had been taken
and their relationship to the rights and freedoms of citizens.

In December, Mr. Hordern, the M.P. from Horsham who
had raised the question of Scientology in 1967, rose in the
House to ask the Secretary of State for Social Services, Mr.
Crossman, if he had any further statement to make on the
practice of Scientology. Mr. Crossman answered that he had
considered either a public inquiry or a white paper, but felt
that for the time being, "the right course is to leave things
as they are," owing to what he felt was the efficacious results
of the publicity attending the activities of the summer. The
M.P. from East Grinstead, Mr. Smith, and his colleague from
Accrington, Mr. Arthur Davidson, expressed disappointment
at this decision. Mr. Crossman answered that his position was
predicated on the fact that "action did not take the form of
prosecution, but merely forbidding foreign nationals to study
and practice Scientology here." It was as if he meant to say
that it was all right for the English to harm themselves—if
that was in fact what Scientology led to, it was their legal
right—and containment seemed the most responsible course
of action.

A curious offshoot of all this is that L. Ron Hubbard, because he is an American citizen, is now *persona non grata* in
England. This does not seem to disturb him at all. Tracked
down recently by a British film team which located the *Apollo*
tied up at a tiny North African port, Hubbard blandly stated,

"In the first place I am not in trouble with the British Government, not even faintly. If I went in today, or tomorrow, through Immigration, they would tip their hats and say, 'How are you, Mr. Hubbard?' as they have been doing for years." Regarding all the criticism of Scientology, he said, "Why do they just fight it and say there's something bad? They never specify what's bad. For instance, right now, they say we're breaking up marriages. Why, that's a lie—" As he said this his intonation lilted, and his voice became full of sweet reason. "As a matter of fact, they're saying that at the moment when you've got this book—" he held up a book to the camera "—which was just about to go on the press: *How to Save Your Marriage.*" Hubbard glanced down at the book, still held to the camera, his whole attitude one bordering on disbelief that Scientology could be causing so much of an uproar back in England. When asked about rumors that he had amassed several million dollars in Swiss bank accounts, Hubbard answered that "one tends to overlook the fact that all during the thirties, and actually during the late forties, I was a highly successful writer, and a great many properties and so on accumulated during that period of time. The amounts of money in Switzerland are minimal. I don't have Swiss bank accounts; there is a bank account in Switzerland. I don't know how much money is in it, but not very much. While there were very, very large sums that I made when I was very young. . . ." He paused to fix his unseen interviewer with a level stare as I, watching his admirably smooth performance, wondered what final saturating generality he would offer to put us all in our places. He said, "Fifteen million published words and a great many successful movies don't make nothing." I wanted to stand up and cheer.

Here he was, twenty years after giving us Dianetics—A.D. 20, he designates this year—and Scientology is shaking people up all over the world: the Australians have banned it in some of their states, the British are going to "look into it" with what

I am sure will be ceremonial probity, Americans are wondering why their kids are flocking to it, and a tiny fleet of ships is throwing a chill over various Mediterranean port authorities as it heaves into view. I remembered the girl I had spoken with at the Scientology Congress, Mary-Lou, and her meaningless statistic that Scientology had grown 500 percent over a very few months. I decided to look into Scientology's growth more closely.

It was already clear to me that Scientology's expansion primarily encompasses the English-speaking world, with twenty-six city centers now spread across England, the U.S., Canada, Australia, New Zealand, South Africa, and Rhodesia. Scientology claims equal success in other countries, but at the present time only three non-English-speaking centers are active, in France, Denmark, and Sweden. The obvious problem for non-English-speaking nationals would be one of language, although Scandinavians study English at school and from my own experience seldom seem at a disadvantage when speaking the language. Scientology hotly disputes the primacy of English, saying that its texts, at least most of them, translate freely and directly into any foreign tongue. One of Hubbard's books, *Scientology: The Fundamentals of Thought*, carries a note at the end of the introduction, which reads: "This text has been organized so that a complete translation of all of it will deliver without interruption or destructive change the basics of Scientology into non-English tongues." I think it's an overly ambitious promise. While Scientology's rampant neologism was part and parcel of making it all valid for people absorbing the meaning of *preclear*, "*thetan*," and "*engram*," the full Hubbardian *meaning* of these and all his other words simply would not translate with ease. A second equally serious consideration for foreigners is that processing and training in a local organization can only be carried up to a certain level. Beyond it, scientologists must go either to Saint Hill, in England—now become difficult, although I've heard Englishmen say that someone determined to get into the country wouldn't really have much trouble—or to Los Angeles. When it became apparent that a scientologist determined to achieve the state of *clear* would have at least some difficulty in getting into England, Scientology set up an advanced organization in Los Angeles, offering both the highly regarded Saint Hill Special Briefing Course, as well as the higher Grades of Release unavailable locally. Hubbard also directed the formation of an Advanced Organization, staffed by members of his elite "Sea Org," to take students beyond the state of *clear* towards becoming that absolute perfection, an *operating thetan*.

I found additional clues as to how many people are in Scientology in figures printed in recent issues of *The Auditor*, Scientology's monthly journal. Discussing the Saint Hill Special Briefing Course, it said that since its inception in April of 1961, 614 students had completed the course, 2001 people have achieved the state of *clear*, and 21,307 have achieved Release. These figures are just for Saint Hill in England, and appear to increase at the rate of 50 persons a month. If you figure that *clear* is the culmination of some twelve grades of advancement, and you allow for *some* attrition, you begin to get some idea of the size of this thing. Bob Thomas, when I talked to him at his New York office, graciously tried to pin it down more precisely. On a worldwide basis, he conservatively estimated, "well over a million people" are now involved, with a central organization of about 100,000 of what he called "card-carrying members." He told me that between one and two hundred new people encounter Scientology for the first time each week in New York alone, and between 50 to 75 percent of them go on to take at least the most elementary course offered, the Communications Course.

We got into the whole subject of costs, either for Scientology processing by itself, or for both it and Scientology training, and how much you might have to lay out to achieve that state of Total Freedom: *clear*. Thomas compared it to the price tag on a medium-priced car. Looking through one of Scientology's brochures, I found the figure broken down more or less as follows: $750 to achieve the first Grades of Release which are called O through IV; $500 to take the Dianetics Auditor's Course; $1,200 to take the Power Grade, Grade V-VA; $775 to take Grade VI, referred to as SOLO because you do it alone; and $800 for Grade VII, *clear*. Power Processing, Grade V-VA, is also offered as a twenty-five-hour intensive, five daily sessions of five hours each at an overall cost of $500, with a minimum of two intensives required. The Saint Hill Special Briefing Course costs $775. At a certain level of processing and training, students are urged to own their own E-Meter, the latest model of which is the Hubbard Mark V E-Meter, sold for $140. Every time I get a new brochure or newsletter from Scientology, I see a new package plan being offered. On something called Triple Flow Grades, people are encouraged to prepay and get a 5 percent discount.

On the training side, there is now a package to take you to Level IV on the Dianetics Auditor's Course for $1,235—5 percent off the usual $1,300 if you pay in advance. There are all kinds of incentive plans offering discounts which range from 5 percent to 50 percent on courses and processes, all of the discounts contingent on your making a long-term commitment—usually by written contract—to follow the upward path of scientological advancement. A free six-month membership in HASI offers a straight 20 percent discount on all Scientology books which normally cost over $1.25, as well as on tapes, records, E-Meters, and other miscellaneous items available from Scientology bookstores, one of which is located in every Scientology office throughout the world. In addition to two pamphlets which sell for 50 cents, there are now eleven books available at $1.25 each, nine books selling for $2.00 each, eleven books selling for $3.00 each, three—among them the original Dianetics text—selling for $5.00, and two selling for $7.00. With only one exception, something called *Miracles for*

*Breakfast,* written by Ruth Minshull, the majority of the books —those which aren't anonymously authored—are written by L. Ron Hubbard. A steady flow of mailings which I—and everybody else in or out of Scientology who happens to be on the mailing lists—received, told me that the books are available and that the bookstore officer was my "terminal for information you may have concerning books." Scientology recently offered an extension course, to be taken at home, for $5.00, consisting of what were called Four Lesson Tablets—"each containing 20 lessons, 8 questions each," each lesson pertaining to one of four books, available at a total cost of $16.25. In addition to the books, scientologists can also buy magazines, charts, the Creed of the Church of Scientology ($.50), a photograph of L. Ron Hubbard—12″ x 15″—a "Study Self-Portrait," pins, car badges, scarves, and ties. Tapes are available at $30 per roll, and a record called "Dianetics Modernized for Scientology Students Practice" which includes Hubbard's personally written instructions costs $15.00. With all these materials, I thought time and time again, is it any wonder that people's immersion in Scientology is total and absolute?

A pertinent curiosity is the picture featured on some of the paperback books which shows an old man, a sad-eyed, white-haired, bearded fellow with unusually flared nostrils. I asked Bob Thomas whether this figure represented anything. "A symbol of knowledge," he said, "and as a symbol it has an impact." I looked again at one of the books, *Introduction to Scientology Ethics,* when I got home. The old man is sitting behind a desk, his arms resting on it. His face is weary, but there was a kind of . . . *timelessness* about it. His robes are black and his left hand is lying lightly on his right. The back of his chair is high and square. He looks like a judge. A wise, stern judge who will brook no nonsense. As I looked at him, I couldn't help remembering a series of stories Hubbard had written many years ago for *Astounding Science Fiction,* using the pen name Rene Lafayette. The stories were called *Soldiers of Light* and told of a time in the future when medicine has become so superior and purified that its practitioners are something akin to superbeings, "soldiers of light." Lafayette's—or Hubbard's—hero in these stories was Old "Doc" Methuselah, a man of enormous insight and sagacity, who, as his name implied, is a thousand years old and blessed with a wisdom accumulated over those centuries.

In discussing the various prices, Minister Thomas was careful to explain that all course costs are on a money-back guarantee and are established by "the Organization." The base rate, if one can call it that, is "$150 per grade of release . . . achieved to the satisfaction of the client," though private practitioners like him have the right to charge more, based, he was not loath to suggest, on what the traffic might bear. "The charge is for a particular result," he explained almost loftily. "In my career I've only had one person who asked for his money back, and I gave it to him."

There is, Thomas went on, "no legal requirement by World-Wide to be franchised. You don't have to be a franchised auditor to be a professional, but most professional auditors desire to be franchised because of the administrative assistance and advices that are given. The requirements are very stringent. You've got to adhere to the policies of Scientology and the ethical codes of Scientology. A professional auditor who is not franchised does not work directly with the organization," but is still "bound by certain codes of ethics." As for the 10 percent which goes to HCO (WW), a professional, nonfranchised auditor may or may not pay it. As Thomas explained, "it's up to them."

Some cities in the U.S., like Chicago, do not have incorporated Scientology churches or organizations. The reason was explained to me by Jack Horner. "An auditor," he said, "can operate under a franchise agreement as long as he doesn't get too big. He gives ten percent of his gross to the organization. That's fair. He's allowed to teach very rudimentary courses.

He operates independently. So this means that an auditor working alone can make anywhere from nothing up to $25,000 a year. This is why the auditors in Chicago don't work in the organization, because the minute you go to work in an organization you go on their so-called Unit System, and this can mean anything from $30 a week, to a top executive who might get $150. The branch office wouldn't be yours any more; it belongs to Hubbard."

I asked Bob Thomas about Hubbard's activities on the *Apollo*, now that he has avowedly severed his connections with the administrative operation of Scientology around the world. "It's like a retreat," Thomas explained, meaning Hubbard's floating domicile, "for advanced Scientologists. Mr. Hubbard is no longer on the board of directors of any of the organizations. He has relinquished everything but being titular head of Scientology," though he "still contributes any technical advances by virtue of research now going on."

Hubbard has, it is true, divested himself of his directorship of the various HASI's and churches, but he is still head of HCO (WW), and, according to Thomas, "ten percent is paid to World-Wide for research, and communications."

Exactly what this research is Hubbard himself explained to the persistent British film crew which had located him and his flagship. "I am studying ancient civilizations," he said, "trying to find out what happened to them, finding out why they went into a decline, why they died." As to his relationship to Scientology today, Hubbard blithely said, "Let's get my relationship to this completely straight: I am the writer of the textbooks of Scientology." Which is nonsense. Hubbard's hand is evident in almost everything happening in Scientology today. Any doubts I might have had were dispelled early this year when I received a "loyalty petition" issued by the Committee For Democratic Mental Practices of the N.A.A.P., P.O. Box 380, New York, N.Y. 10024. Twelve years after his ridiculous "loyalty oath" which he mailed out to psychologists, psychiatrists, psychoanalysts, and "ministers of various denominations who engage in mental practice," here was that old National Academy of American Psychology sending out this incredible petition which begins: "It is not generally appreciated in the United States that the field of mental healing could be used by a foreign power to undermine our democratic system of government." What follows is a rhetorical treatise on how malpractice in the mental sciences is being used under our very noses to subvert . . . you name it: individuals, organizations, the whole country! The petition to be tendered Congress states "that every person engaged in the treatment of mental illness, including psychiatrists, psychologists and psychotherapists in the United States and its protectorates, shall solumnly [sic] declare before any Justice of the Peace that he is not a member of any movement or party, nor is he associated with, for fee or reward, any foreign power or organization which has as its aim the undermining or subversion of the Constitution or elected government of the United States of America." It is a sickening piece of tripe and smells of that age-old giveaway: somebody or something running scared.

A much more personal glimpse of what Hubbard is up to was given by Nick Robinson, a young Englishman who had spent months aboard the *Royal Scot Man* and finally left, bitterly disillusioned. Speaking in a slightly hesitant, carefully pointed manner, he told the British film team whose work I was able to screen, that Hubbard "really is in charge, all the way. He used to use Telexes every day from his organizations all over the world, especially Saint Hill in England. And he sends Telexes to Saint Hill, gives them instructions and so on and so on. So he really is involved. On board the ship he's a kind of Jesus Christ-cum-Buddha all rolled into one. His busts and photographs are everywhere. He just is God."

# TWO

# THE REAL TRUTH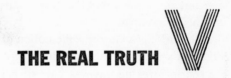

The substance of what Scientology proposes as the truth about life, existence, and the condition of man is infinitely more complex than those rather crude Dianetics concepts about an *analytical* mind, a *reactive* mind, and the existence of traceable engrams. All of L. Ron Hubbard's frantic comings and goings were "firmly" based on a genuine philosophy which he had put together, a philosophy which combined, with typically billowing grandeur, the highest aspirations of pure Eastern thinking and the meanest invention of the best science-fiction bravado. Before I can explain the techniques this daring man developed for the achievement of both the knowledge and states of enlightenment he offers, we have to tackle exactly what Scientology says it believes.

If I were to call L. Ron Hubbard eclectic, it would be a mild understatement. The foreword of one of his early books, *Scientology 8-8008*, acknowledges a debt to Sigmund Freud, as well as someone Hubbard claims to have met in the Navy, a Commander Thompson who was supposedly one of Freud's pupils. The foreword then goes on to list a few other people Hubbard feels he should credit as the source for his ideas: Anaxagoras, Aristotle, Roger Bacon—the acknowledgment is in alphabetical order—Buddha, Charcot, Confucius, René Descartes, Will Durant, Euclid, Michael Faraday, William James, Thomas Jefferson, Jesus of Nazareth, Count Alfred Korzybski, James Clerk Maxwell, Mohammed, Lao Tsze, van Leeuwenhoek,

Lucretius, Isaac Newton, Thomas Paine, Plato, Socrates, Herbert Spencer, the Vedic Hymns, and Voltaire. The implication is clear: Not only is Hubbard well read and immensely discerning, but he himself may deserve a place among such august and heady company.

Hubbard has a very specific notion of where, in the progression and scheme of things, Scientology belongs. In an outline for the lectures he gave as part of Scientology's Professional Course in July of 1954, he blocked out the earlier forms of wisdom which preceded Scientology. He began with the Veda, the sacred Hindu literature, and then moved to the Tao, the thinking of Lao-Tsze and "The principle of wu-wei (non-assertion or non-compulsion) control by permitting self-determinism." This was followed by the Dhyana, a discussion of its source, and the introduction of Gautama Sakyamundi, with extensive quotes from the Dharmapada, verses attributed to Sakyamundi who was considered the founder of the Dhyana. From there Hubbard moved on to the Hebrews and their definition of the Messiah. Then to Jesus of Nazareth, his age, his teaching and healing, his use of parables, his principles of love and compassion amongst peoples, and his Crucifixion. From there Hubbard discussed the spread of Christianity into "The Barbarism of Europe: Religion with fur breech-clouts," the closing of the trade routes, and the appearance of "Western Seekers of Wisdom." His lectures ended with Webster's definition of religion, and the qualification that a religion or religious philosophy had as its goal "the freeing of the soul by wisdom," a goal achieved by Scientology.

Hubbard had, as was mentioned earlier, already lectured on his ideas concerning the *theta*, man's true spirit, and MEST, the product of *theta* in the form of matter, energy, space, and time, as early as late 1950. Codifying his thinking further, he stated what he believed to be a basic truth in a book called *The Creation of Human Ability*. "*Considerations,*" he wrote, "*take rank over the mechanics of space, energy, and time. By* this it is meant that an idea or opinion is, fundamentally, superior to space, energy, and time, or organizations of form, since it is conceived that space, energy, and time are themselves broadly agreed-upon considerations. That so many minds agree brings about Reality in the form of space, energy, and time. These mechanics, then, of space, energy, and time are the products of agreed-upon considerations mutually held by life."

"Reality," John McMasters had said in his talk, "is *agreement*." Everything Scientology postulates is based upon this one idea. Everything said thus becomes valid and acquires its own importance, its own existence as a *consideration*. What this means further is that every idea Hubbard then introduced might very well be absolutely true. His problem was first to define what it was he had discovered to be the truth, and then develop a way through which his followers could achieve the same revelations and states of enlightenment.

The evolution of Hubbard's achievement of his many *considerations* first appeared in print in 1951, in a book called *Science of Survival*. In it he explained that all life is composed of two elements: statics and kinetics. A static was that which possessed no motion and was without width, length, breadth, depth, and mass. Its capabilities were unlimited, and it could be represented by the mathematical symbol *theta* ($\theta$). The kinetic he called MEST, the physical universe in terms of matter, energy, space, and time. In *Scientology 8-8008* he summarized all this as follows: "It is now considered that the origin of MEST lies with *theta* itself, and that MEST, as we know the physical universe, is a product of *theta*." Put another way, colloquially, all matter, energy, space, and time are, well, a figment of our imagination. *It* is all here because we are thinking *it*.

It is important to understand what the *theta* and its entity the *thetan* has represented to Hubbard over the years, because what it is, how it has behaved, and why, have produced many of the *considerations* fundamental to Scientology. After naming it in *Science of Survival*, Hubbard, in *Scientology 8-80* (a book which appeared in 1952 and not to be confused with a subsequent book, *Scientology 8-8008*) gave more information concerning the *thetan*.

> *Thetan*, [he wrote] is the word given to the awareness of awareness unit, the life source, the personality, and the beingness of homo sapiens. . . . It is the person. . . . The *thetan* is a glowing unit of energy source. He seems to himself to be anything from a quarter of an inch to two inches in diameter. His capability is knowing and being. He exudes and uses energy in many forms. He can perceive and handle energy flows easily. The *thetan* enters some time in early infancy. This may be before, during or following birth. He comes in a state of personal unknowingness, desiring to have an identity which he considers he has not without a body. He throws capping beams at the genetic entity, takes over the body. . . .

The "genetic entity" (GE) which had a "capping beam" thrown over it by the *thetan* is, according to Hubbard's explanation, something akin to a trace memory from a thetan's very first MEST body. It appears somewhere in the body's center, vaguely in the area of the stomach, and was what Dianetics had once identified as being the somatic mind. The GE, Hubbard wrote, "carries on through the evolutionary parallel with the protoplasmic line, generation to generation, usually on the same planet."

The *thetan* may be extraterrestrial and has certainly been elsewhere, galactically speaking, but the GE has been on this planet from the very beginning of time.

> The genetic entity apparently enters the protoplasm line some two days or a week prior to conception. There is some evidence that the GE is actually double, one entering on the sperm side, one entering on the ovum side. . . . Pre-sperm recordings are quite ordinary. . . . Pre-ovum sequences are on record but are not common. . . . The *theta* being apparently joins the track immediately prior to birth. Its sequence, for

itself, is death, between-lives, birth, all in a few minutes according to some findings, a sequence which is quite aberrative. . . . The genetic line consists of the total of incidents which have occurred during the evolution of the MEST body itself. The composite of these facsimiles has the semblance of being [i.e., the GE. Discovering it, Hubbard wrote] makes it possible at last to vindicate the theory of evolution proposed by Darwin. . . . You as a *theta* being may or may not have seen Greece or Rome. Your MEST GE has probably activated a body there, just as it has been . . . an anthropoid in the deep forests of forgotten continents or a mollusc seeking to survive on the shore of some lost sea.

For eons, the GE progressed, first as a clam, then as something Hubbard called the "Grim Weeper," or "Boohoo," an entity which "spent half a million years on the beach," struggling to breathe, desperate to eat, opening up for food and instead getting an incoming wave in its mouth. The water would be pumped out, and the weeper was in action. Time passed. The GE was involved as a bird, or a bat, was eaten, was a sloth—terrified of snakes and of falling—became a caveman, and even Piltdown man—the now famous prehistoric-man hoax—who became responsible for "obsessions about biting, efforts to hide the mouth and early familial troubles" because "the Piltdown teeth were enormous and he was quite careless as to whom and what he bit and often very surprised at the resulting damage."

The importance of the GE has been somewhat downgraded by Scientology in recent years, although its presence and effect is still acknowledged. The qualities and capabilities of the *thetan* have always been much more important. They are what Scientology sees as being the optimum expression of what we all really are: telepathy, psychokinetic powers, emission of electronic flow, exteriorization. . . . "A *theta* body," Hubbard wrote, "with its alertness restored is capable of remolding the human body within its field, taking off weight here, restoring it there, changing appearances and even height."

Going hand in hand with Hubbard's "discovery" of the existence of the *theta* was his doctrine concerning "past lives," where the *theta* had made extraordinary voyages and undergone startling adventures, all of which play an important role in determining the health and welfare of the *theta* in whatever state it is in at a given moment. Since time began, *theta* has been acquiring and losing bodies, some on this earth, some elsewhere. The moment of acquiring a new body is a moment of unknowingness for the *thetan,* and though the new body functions, its identity is a mystery. Thus, in Scientology's christening ceremony, the *thetan* meets its own body as well as the bodies of those adults whom it can depend on for care and feeding.

Once life or involvement with a body ends for a *thetan,* it leaves it, making its way directly to what is called an Implant Station, there to be implanted with various goals, the most common of which is the goal To Forget. At the implant station, the *thetan* waits to pick up another body. There is often competition among the *thetans* gathered there because it seems that being a *thetan* without a body is uncomfortable. The minimum time spent waiting, according to Hubbard, is sixty-nine days. Hubbard has said that on a visit to Venus he toured an Implant Station, though there are other such stations located throughout the universe. "The report area for most has been Mars," he wrote in *A History of Man.* "Some women report to stations elsewhere in the Solar System. There are occasional incidents about Earth report stations. The report stations are protected by screens. The last report station on Earth was established in the Pyrenees."

With these preliminary beliefs established, there are certain essential "certainties," or abstracts which we should get into here because they affect the way Scientology examines the universe and then seeks to explain why what happens happens in a particular way, and why behavior occurs in a particular way.

Scientology's foundation stone is "the CYCLE OF ACTION," which Hubbard described in *Scientology: The Fundamentals of Thought*. He began by defining the ancient, traditional cycle of birth springing from chaos: growing, decaying, dying, and returning to chaos. This, he said, Scientology expressed "more briefly. The CYCLE OF ACTION IS AN APPARENCY AS FOLLOWS: CREATE, then SURVIVE, then DESTROY; or Creation, Survival, Destruction." The word APPARENCY is important here because according to Hubbard this cycle is an *idea* which we believe to be so because we see it. We suppose it to be so—CONSIDER it—and "then we see it so." He then takes the traditional life-cycle of birth, life, and death, and says, "In Scientology it can be seen that none of these steps are necessary. One considers them so, and so they are 'true.' A man . . . grows old to the degree that he believes he is growing old." His point is that our agreement makes this cycle be so, but, he adds, it "is not TRUE. It is only APPARENT. It is APPARENT because we believe we see it . . . because we AGREE that it should be so." Arguing that our belief in this particular "cycle of action" has never cured anyone of anything, or made them more intelligent, Hubbard suggests that the cycle must obviously be wrong. He then suggests that all of the elements of this particular cycle are, in fact, creative acts. Here is how he charts what he means:

> CREATE=make, manufacture, construct, postulate, bring into beingness=CREATE.
>
> Create-create-create=create again continuously one moment after the next=SURVIVAL.
>
> Create-counter-create=to create something against a creation— to create one thing and then create something else against= DESTROY.
>
> No creation=an absence of any creation=no creative activity.

These principles are absolutely fundamental to Hubbard's thinking and play a crucial role in the development of the techniques for the achievement of Scientology's enlightenment.

When Hubbard developed Dianetics, he postulated four dynamics. In Scientology, these expanded to eight, because, "as one looks out across the confusion which is life or existence to most people, one can discover eight main divisions to each of which applies the condition of existence. Each division contains a cycle of action." The eight dynamics are:

THE FIRST DYNAMIC—is the urge toward existence as one's self. Here we have individuality expressed fully. This can be called the SELF DYNAMIC.

THE SECOND DYNAMIC—is the urge toward existence as a sexual or bisexual activity. This dynamic actually has two divisions. Second Dynamic (a) is the sexual act itself and the Second Dynamic (b) is the family unit, including the rearing of children. This can be called the SEX DYNAMIC.

THE THIRD DYNAMIC—is the urge toward existence in groups of individuals. Any group or part of an entire class could be considered to be a part of the Third Dynamic. The school, the society, the town, the nation are each part of the Third Dynamic, and each one is a Third Dynamic. This can be called the GROUP DYNAMIC.

THE FOURTH DYNAMIC—is the urge toward mankind. Whereas the white race would be considered a Third Dynamic, all the races would be considered the Fourth Dynamic. This can be called the MANKIND DYNAMIC.

THE FIFTH DYNAMIC—is the urge toward existence of the animal kingdom. This includes all living things whether vegetable or animal. The fish in the sea, the beasts of the field, or of the forest, grass, trees, flowers or anything directly and intimately motivated by life. This can be called the ANIMAL DYNAMIC.

THE SIXTH DYNAMIC—is the urge toward existence as the physical universe. The physical universe is composed of matter, energy, space and time. In Scientology we take the first of each of these words and coin a word, MEST. This can be called the UNIVERSE DYNAMIC.

THE SEVENTH DYNAMIC—is the urge toward existence as or of spirits. Anything spiritual, with or without identity, would come under the heading of the Seventh Dynamic. This can be called the SPIRITUAL DYNAMIC.

THE EIGHTH DYNAMIC—is the urge toward existence as

Infinity. This is also identified as the Supreme Being. It is carefully observed here that the *science* of Scientology does not intrude into the Dynamic of the Supreme Being. This is called the Eighth Dynamic because the symbol of infinity stood upright makes the numeral "8." This can be called the INFINITY or GOD DYNAMIC.

"The keystone of living associations," Hubbard wrote in *Scientology: The Fundamentals of Thought,* is "The ARC triangle." He called it life's "common denominator." The A stands for Affinity in the sense of emotions such as loving or liking. The R represents Reality, that which people agree is real. The C is Communications, the most important of the triangle's three corners because it is "the solvent for all things." Hubbard explains that a communication must consist of something to send to someone who is prepared to receive it. And when people have something in common, the same level of "affinity," why communication is simple. But he points out that as we go lower on the "tone scale" our affinities become more solid, so while on the high levels our communications are erudite and friendly, on the bottom you find that most solid of solids: WAR. "Where the affinity level is hate," he tells us coldly, "the agreement is solid matter, and the communication . . . bullets."

This tone scale which Hubbard mentions first appeared in Dianetics is a classification of human emotions in a particular order, from the very bottom—apathy—to the very top—enthusiasm. Each level was given a number and arranged in a descending order of desirability. What was important was not the particular number opposite an emotion, but that it was either higher or lower—better or worse—than another emotion.

The tone scale, Hubbard wrote, "plots the descending spiral of life from full vitality and consciousness through half vitality and half consciousness down to death . . . the whole intent of Scientology is to raise the individual from lower to higher strata on this scale by increasing intelligence, awareness, and ability."

(The tone scale is diagramed on the following page.)

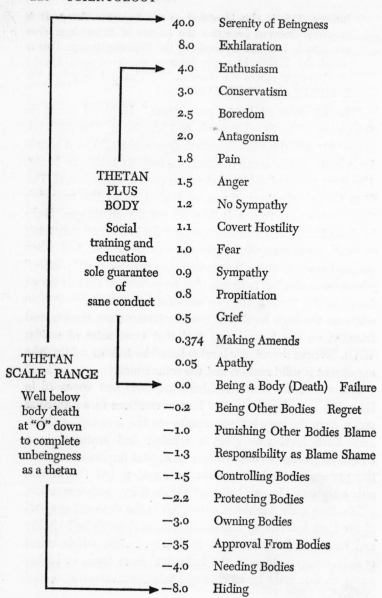

| | | |
|---|---|---|
| | 40.0 | Serenity of Beingness |
| | 8.0 | Exhilaration |
| | 4.0 | Enthusiasm |
| | 3.0 | Conservatism |
| | 2.5 | Boredom |
| | 2.0 | Antagonism |
| | 1.8 | Pain |
| THETAN PLUS BODY | 1.5 | Anger |
| | 1.2 | No Sympathy |
| Social training and education sole guarantee of sane conduct | 1.1 | Covert Hostility |
| | 1.0 | Fear |
| | 0.9 | Sympathy |
| | 0.8 | Propitiation |
| | 0.5 | Grief |
| | 0.374 | Making Amends |
| THETAN SCALE RANGE | 0.05 | Apathy |
| | 0.0 | Being a Body (Death)    Failure |
| Well below body death at "O" down to complete unbeingness as a thetan | —0.2 | Being Other Bodies    Regret |
| | —1.0 | Punishing Other Bodies  Blame |
| | —1.3 | Responsibility as Blame Shame |
| | —1.5 | Controlling Bodies |
| | —2.2 | Protecting Bodies |
| | —3.0 | Owning Bodies |
| | —3.5 | Approval From Bodies |
| | —4.0 | Needing Bodies |
| | —8.0 | Hiding |

At the same time that Scientology's intention is to raise a person on the tone scale and improve his abilities, it is also Scientology's goal to rehabilitate the *thetan* by removing aberrations. This is critical because if it can be done successfully during this lifetime, the *thetan* will enjoy all future lives free of any kind of problems. If, however, aberrations are only "keyed out," which is merely being released from some portion of the reactive mind, the death of the current body—Scientologists often refer to our bodies as "this piece of meat," or "this meat of ours"—will not free the *thetan* from suffering the reappearance of aberrations. Furthermore, a properly freed *thetan* will not have to return to an implant station to obtain a new body. So Scientology's techniques locate the *thetan* and bring its past experiences out into the open. Like Dianetics, there was one aberration which was absolutely "basic" to the liberation of the *thetan*. "The one basic engram," as Hubbard described it in *Scientology 8-80*, "on top of which all this-life engrams are mere locks . . . was received by the human race many, many centuries ago, and probably was a supersonic shot in the forehead, chest, and stomach, incapacitating, and reducing, the size and function of the pineal gland."

It was a major "breakthrough" in Scientology when Hubbard announced that the actual sources of aberrations for the *thetan* were the implants themselves. During a *thetan's* sojourn at an implant station the goal To Forget was implanted, and all during previous lives, the *thetan* was having a wide variety of other goals implanted. Thus trapped by this goal To Forget, it became a monumental task to unlock those goals which had been over-implanted by the goal To Forget. This particular goal, according to Hubbard, was implanted on the planet Helatrobus some 38 trillion to 43 trillion years ago. In an HCO Bulletin, July 24, 1963, Hubbard described other implants which had been perpetrated upon *thetans* prior to the Helatrobus Implants.

| | |
|---|---|
| Helatrobus Implants | 38.2 trillion years ago to 52 trillion years ago. |
| Aircraft Door Implants | 216 trillion years ago to 315 trillion years ago. |
| The Gorilla Goals | 319 trillion years ago to 83 trillion trillion trillion years ago. |
| The Bear Goals | 83 trillion trillion trillion years ago to about 40.7 trillion trillion trillion trillion years ago. |
| The Glade Implants (*formerly called Black Thetan*) | 40.7 trillion trillion trillion trillion years ago to 5.9 trillion trillion trillion trillion trillion years ago. |
| The Invisible Picture Goals | 5.9 trillion trillion trillion trillion trillion to a date not fully determined. |
| The Minion Implants | Not yet determined. |
| The Story of Creation Implants | 70 trillion trillion trillion trillion trillion trillion trillion years. |

Ten days earlier, in an HCO Bulletin dated July 14, 1963, Hubbard revealed in fascinating detail how some of the various goals were "laid in." The Aircraft Goal "was given in the mocked up fuselage of an aircraft with the *thetan* fixed before an aircraft door. . . ." The Gorilla Goals were

> given in an amusement park with a single tunnel, a roller coaster and a ferris wheel. . . . The symbol of a Gorilla was always present in the place the goal was given. Sometimes a large gorilla, black, was seen elsewhere than the park. A Mechanical or live gorilla was always seen in the park. This activity was conducted by the Hoipolloi, a group of operators in meat body societies. They were typical carnival people. They let out Concessions for these Implant "Amusement Parks." A pink-striped white shirt with sleeve garters was the uniform of the Hoipolloi. Such a figure often rode on the roller coaster cars. Monkeys were also used on the cars. Elephants sometimes formed part of the equipment. The Hoipolloi or Gorilla goals were laid in with fantastic motion.

Blasts of raw electricity and explosions were both used to lay
the Items in. [The Black Thetan goals] were given in a glade
surrounded by the stone heads of "black thetans" who spat
white energy at the trapped thetan. The trapped thetan was
motionless.

Of course all this struck me as being insane garbage. While
the wordy repostulations of affinity, reality, and communications, and the cycles of action and the dynamics were all
something I could swallow simply because they were primarily
the taking of existing concepts or notions or even relationships
and rewording them, giving them new names, so that you
would see them *his* way, the Goals struck me as being pure
science fiction. Talking to a Scientologist one day, trying hard
to maintain objectivity and an open mind, I suddenly blurted
out that believing in something like the Gorilla Goals was
stretching it. The scientologist looked mildly surprised. "Why?"
he said.

"*Gorilla* Goals?" I shot back.

"Well," he said thoughtfully, "I might have agreed at one
time, except that a couple of months ago I got this bad
toothache. And I knew there was no *reason* for me to have it;
I'd gone to the dentist and there was nothing wrong with my
teeth. So I sat down and thought about why I had this toothache. And all of a sudden, I saw a gorilla."

"A gorilla?"

The scientologist smiled, almost apologetically. "I know how
that sounds. But I did. I saw this very big gorilla."

". . . Because your toothache had something to do with a
goal connected to the time you were a gorilla, or something?"
I said.

"Something like that," the scientologist said calmly.

The weird thing is that just at this point, where Hubbard
runs the risk of really losing me, he combines a couple of
these elements to produce yet another principle which is not
wildly fanciful.

The idea that your having a goal-created energy which had actual mass led him to define something he called GPM: "goals-problems-mass." The idea quite simply was that in past lives a person acquired, one way or another, pleasantly or unpleasantly, a wide variety of goals, all of varying natures of importance. But each, because it was a goal, acquired certain obstacles it had to overcome. Problems arose, and as such, as the mind or *theta* grappled with these problems, mass accumulated. It may have been solely in the form of stored-up energy, but it was definitely mass, and it was, according to Hubbard, measurable. In a book called *Dianetics: 1955*, Hubbard had written: "If there were no energy being created by the awareness-of-awareness unit (the *thetan*), then one would be at a loss to account for mental energy pictures, for these things, being made at a tremendously rapid rate, have considerable mass in them—mass which is measurable on a thing which is as common and everyday as a pair of bathroom scales." The E-Meter.

In what I humbly would have to call an astounding revelation made known in an HCO Bulletin of May 11, 1963, known as the "Heaven" bulletin, L. Ron Hubbard announced that GPM implants had been done in Heaven. "The contents of this HCO Bulletin," he wrote, "discover the apparent underlying impulses of religious zealotism and the source of the religious mania and insanity which terrorized Earth over the ages and has given religion the appearance of insanity." In no uncertain terms, he explained why and how the implants occurred. "For a long while, some people have been cross with me for my lack of co-operation in believing in a Christian Heaven, God and Christ. I have never said I didn't disbelieve in a Big Thetan but there was certainly something very corny about Heaven *et al*. Now I have to apologize. There was a Heaven. Not too unlike, in cruel betrayal, the heaven of the Assassins in the 12th Century, who, like everyone else, dramatized the whole track implants—if a bit more so. . . . The symbol of the crucified Christ is very apt indeed. It's the symbol of a *thetan* betrayed. . . ." Hubbard knew this because he had visited Heaven twice. "The first time I arrived and the moment of the implant To Forget was dated at 43,891,611,177 years, 344 days, 10 hours, 20 minutes and 40 seconds from 10:02½ P.M. Daylight Greenwich Time May 9, 1963. The second series was dated to the moment of the implant To Forget as 42,681,459,477,315 years, 132 days, 18 hours, 20 minutes and 15 seconds from 11:02½ P.M. Daylight Greenwich Time May 19, 1963." The implants, Hubbard wrote, were electronic and done on a nonvisible *thetan* who arrived by ship in a doll's body. Twenty-nine goals were made the first visit, 21 the second. Each time the first three goals were identical: To Forget, To Remember, To Go Away.

All of what Scientology believes and theorizes can, Hubbard explains in *The Creation of Human Ability*, be broadly divided into two general categories: Scientology and Para-Scientology.

Under Scientology we group those things of which we can be certain and only those things of which we can be certain. . . . Para-Scientology is that large bin which includes all greater or lesser uncertainties. Here are the questionable things, the things of which the common normal observer cannot be sure with a little study. Here are theories, here are groups of data, even groups commonly accepted as "known." Some of the classified bodies of data which fall in Para-Scientology are: Dianetics, incidents on the "wholetrack," the immortality of Man, the existence of God, engrams containing pain and unconsciousness and yet all perception, prenatals, clears, character, and many other things which, even when closely and minutely observed, still are not certain things to those who observe them. Such things have relative truth. They have to some a high degree of reality; they have to others nonexistence. They require a highly specialized system in order to observe them at all. Working with such uncertainties one can produce broad and sweeping results: one can make the ill well again, one can right even the day which went most wrong; but those things which require highly specialized communication systems remain uncertain to many. . . . Also under the heading of Para-Scientology one would place such things as past lives, mysterious influences, astrology, mysticism, religion, psychology, psychiatry, nuclear physics, and any other science based on theory.

Rather than be any sort of refutation of Scientology's beliefs and theories, the notion of a Scientology and a Para-Scientology confounds only because with continued development of various avenues of thinking, it became increasingly difficult to separate what was a concrete Scientological "consideration," and what represented Para-Scientology's "highly specialized system in order to observe them at all." That there is no true division between the two categories is evident from the Axioms, which represent the fundamental substance of all which Scientology believes, and which Hubbard calls "commonly held considerations."

In all, there are 58 Axioms, 7 Pre-logics, and 24 Logics. They range from Axiom 1: "LIFE IS BASICALLY A STATIC," to Axiom 39: "LIFE POSES PROBLEMS FOR ITS OWN SOLUTION," to Axiom 48: "LIFE IS A GAME WHEREIN THETA AS THE STATIC SOLVES THE PROBLEMS OF THETA AS MEST." Pre-logic 1 is: "SELF-DETERMINISM IS THE COMMON DENOMINATOR OF ALL LIFE IMPULSES." LOGIC 18 is: "A POSTULATE IS AS VALUABLE AS IT IS WORKABLE."

I have already pointed out that in explaining the origin of the word Scientology, Hubbard never mentioned the German social psychologist, Dr. A. Nordenholz. Nor does Hubbard acknowledge any possible debt to Nordenholz in his extensive listings of his researches into Eastern and Western thinking. But Nordenholz is important.

Very little is known about this man who wrote several books which examine the social phenomenon of the individual against the concept of the "self" as created by the conscious mind. He was born in Buenos Aires in 1862, the son of the German consul there, and returned to his fatherland where he became a farmer, scientist, Doctor of Law and Philosophy, and was interested in the links binding economic and social problems both in the question of industrial production and in the question of social identities. In 1904, he joined Dr. Alfred Ploetz to found a periodical in Germany called *The Racial, Social, Biological Archive, Including Racial and Social Hygiene.* It was published regularly until July of 1944, and though Dr. Nordenholz's contributions disappear during the 1920's, it has been speculated that the Archive was an important source of much of the racial thinking of Hitler Germany. In 1934, Nordenholz published a book called *Scientologie: Wissenschaft von der Beschaffenheit und der Tauglichkeit des Wissens (The Science of the Constitution & Usefulness of Knowledge and Knowing).* It was painstakingly and faithfully translated into English recently by Woodward R. McPheeters.

Nordenholz begins by stating that the problem of a science of knowing or knowledge, which he names Scientologie or Eidologie, is isolating knowledge as "a particular appearance of the world." "What is Knowing?" he goes on to ask. "What IS Knowledge? What can we know, what must we know about Knowledge/Knowing, to do justice to and to justify the world? The question is thus nothing less than self-knowing, determination of the nature of self, and also of self-realization and self-understanding of Knowledge/Knowing. Is this possible? If possible, how can the systemization of Knowledge/Knowing itself be accomplished? How can a Science of Knowledge/ Knowing be produced?"

Nordenholz goes on to establish certain definitions and concludes that "the world is nothing but knowledge, merely an extraction from knowing. . . . Only out of the equally valued mutual operation of Knowledge/Knowing as shaper &

creator, and world as created & shaped, is it possible to arrive at the true science of the world. . . . Out of this circumstance comes the right of Scientologie to treat the world as belonging to its counterpart, as an appendage of the consciousness."

Having thus established the relationship between knowledge/knowing and the world, Nordenholz declares that "Unaware thinking within the world has always simply perceived THE state or current condition." He explains that consciousness can be raised to a position of independence, or isolation, and then states: "The consciousness, which always remains a part and particular creation of the world, is incompetent to create from a nothingness because of this very worldliness. In order for the consciousness to be able to create, it has to first find a fountainhead source out of which it can create, and this Something is a Beingness."

Nordenholz next introduces the notion of Axioms as a decreed system to get out of a cycle he identifies as: "the systemization of consciousness & reason demands knowing . . ." versus "knowing demands a system of consciousness & reason." He defines axioms as "comprehensions, propositions, declarations, which are initially set in place *as if* they stand of their own power and dignity, *as if* they were capable of, but do not need, a verification or confirmation from another source." He then goes on to structure Scientologie as follows:

1. In axioms: exposition of the axioms and the axiom systems of consciousness.

2. In systems: erection of the forming or moulding system of the consciousnesses, the comprehension system of the reason, all form the axiom system.

3. In demonstration: justification of the produced comprehension systems and with that, working back to the underlying basis of the axiom systems.

4. In study of the origin, nature, methods, and limits of knowledge: establishment of the Total-system of sciences from the foundation of Scientologie systems of knowledge and comprehension.

The most important axiom, to appreciate Nordenholz's possible influence on L. Ron Hubbard, was the Axiom of Mediation: "The consciousness, nominated as the creator of the world, presupposes a wellspring, a source, out of which it can scoop; a Being, which somehow and in some measure can be reached thru consciousness, but which exists there by itself BEFORE and independent from the consciousness. The assumption of a creator activity of the consciousness is dependent upon the Standing Orders of self-primordial, free, detached, absolute Beings, the By-Itself-Being(s)."

What interested Nordenholz was the eventual relationship between an individual and what is called "society": how his role is defined, how his productivity is affected, what freedom actually means, how power is achieved. If the exposition of all these ideas is difficult and often bordering on the unreadable, it is in part because prior to this, no one had ever attempted to organize a system of thought on the principle that knowledge/knowing might be isolated as an entity called "beingness."

To understand L. Ron Hubbard and Scientology, it is not necessary to suggest he knew of the Nordenholz book and borrowed freely; it is only important to know that Nordenholz had attempted, as early as 1927, to establish a working thesis with regard to what he called "the systemization of consciousness. . . ." Here was the notion of the existence of a "fountainhead source out of which it (consciousness) can create," here was the requirement that "all our comprehensions have to fit themselves into the axiomatically founded system." If Hubbard did in fact know of Nordenholz and his theories, the only thing lacking for him would have been a sense of adventure, of extraterrestrial panache to suggest that what this Beingness might be is something extremely attractive and powerful. For this, he might have found ample inspiration in a book written in 1938 by R. Buckminster Fuller, father of geodesic structures, called *Nine Chains to the Moon*.

*Nine Chains to the Moon* is a long book composed of forty-three brief chapters, each with a snappy title such as "$E = Mc^2 =$ Mrs. Murphy's Horse Power." Each is an expository statement about some aspect of life on this earth, written in a style which is quixotic and hard-hitting, made graphic by extensive use of capitalized words, with whiz-bang conversions of complex abstractions: "The *principle of teleology* implies that the *adequacy and effect of conclusion are directly proportional to the degree of ramification and penetration of the original inclusion*"—into everyday metaphors: "The consumption and digestion of facts and statistics is somewhat like eating and chewing hay and thistles. There is nourishment in them in their raw state, to be sure, but a cow is needed to convert them into milk." All of it is based on a premise which Fuller explains in An Outline: "The sum-total of human desire to survive is dominant over the sum-total of the impulse to destroy." After discussing industry and machinery and Henry Ford and the appearance of alloys and our industrial conceptualization of houses and objects devoid of any insights into the higher meanings of existence, suffering only to protect, maintain and abet life, Fuller tells a short story involving "Mr. Jones . . . an amateur hyper-short wave radio expert, *and* a lovely young lady from XK-planet."

After meeting the young lady, and learning of her planet and its distance from the earth and how XK time is bogglingly different from our time, Jones asks about the X-ian philosophy.

> "First [the young lady says in answer] we evolved a completely ABSTRACTED, DEPERSONALIZED, UN-SELFED BIBLE, which is a rationalized account of the GAME OF LIFE, segregating its *Unity of totality* into *chaotic multiplicity* and subsequently *rationally recomposing* it to *unity*, to *symmetry* of *unity* and to *completeness* through *synchronization*, which is the *checkmating* of *time*, against which the game is played by the totality of TRUE COMPREHENSION."
>
> This attitude [wrote Fuller] caused Jones to realize with astonishment that his earth Bible, through its mysteriously

confused insistence upon explaining the reality of truth in terms of grossly imperfect interpretation of the tangible man mechanism, constantly provokes inability to explain the logically superman realities of totality; with the result that, in terms of the imperfect self mechanism, understanding of the realities has to be unreasonably recognized by a SURRENDERING BELIEF IN MIRACLES, these miracles in turn evoking an awe-ful, fear-ful, wide-eyed, secretive, cultish herding around SECRET THEORIES OF EXPLANATION OF REALITY in the TERMS OF UNREALITY, which, thought Jones, is certainly no fun.

After explaining the game of life, the young lady then went on to explain the X-IAN Resolution. The Resolution is long, goes on for several pages, and is written in that same pounding, all-caps declamatory style. "RESOLVED," it opens, "to solve agelong problems NOW in terms of self instead of egotistically blaming primary cause on some *other thing or being*, simply saying to ourselves: SELF! YOU CAN ONLY BE HURT IF, WHERE, and WHEN YOU ARE VULNERABLE." The Resolution goes on to state that all existence is, in effect, an assumption. Jones and the young lady finally *understand* each other and achieve *communication*.

All this background is basic to what Scientology purports to believe and practice as its tenets. Its intention is to produce at first a *preclear,* formerly called a Mest Clear; then a *clear,* formerly called a *theta clear* and finally, penultimately, an *operating thetan.* The difference between the last two is very important. A *clear* is someone who is *at cause* over matter, energy, space, and time. "In the mental sense," Church of Scientology Minister Bob Thomas emphasized when we discussed Scientology's various states of being.

What Scientology means by the phrase *at cause*, with its companion number, *at effect*, is simply that if something is bothering you, if you are tormented by whatever kind of inner aberration, you must not treat it symptomatically, which is *at effect*—the aberration's effect on you—but where it really began, *at cause.* "When you're clear," Thomas said, "you're free in the mental sense, but you want to extend your influence and power and so on." Thus becoming an *operating thetan* is not merely being *at cause* mentally, but "at cause over matter, energy, space, and time in the *physical,* total sense." When I suggested that this implied that an *operating thetan* could levitate, rise right up into the air and hang there, Thomas sat forward in his chair and said, "Right. These are the ultimate goals that are *envisioned.* I'm saying that these are the ultimate things it is hoped man is capable of; if he really has those potentials, which we assume he has. One of the basic Scientology viewpoints is that absolutes are not attainable in the physical universe, but you can get more and more and more free, and that's what's happening in Scientology: people are finding out more and more about themselves, and the more they find out about themselves, the freer they are. And we envision no ultimate limitation on how free an individual can be. Beyond the state of clear, there are these grades of operating thetans. When you're *clear,* you're free in the mental sense, but you want to extend your influence and power as a spiritual being. And that road is a higher road which Mr. Hubbard is researching at this moment."

# TECHNIQUES, DRILLS, AND PROCESSES

I first encountered both auditing and the structure of Scientology's extensive technology when I was given some simple auditing by a Scientology staff member. It was part of a standard introductory session which had begun with the free Hubbard film and lecture. When it finally came time for me to be audited, actually to see an E-Meter and have it demonstrated on me, the moment, despite the monotony of the film and lecture which had come first, became heavy with meaning, as if *now*, having survived the film and lecture, the inner door was going to open and the heart and substance of Scientology revealed in a clear light.

I was led to a small room by a Miss Adler, a pleasant-looking, large lady who, as I was already getting used to with scientologists, insisted on glaring at me from beneath lowered brows. The room we entered was small and I was made to sit down on one side of a small table. Miss Adler sat down opposite me. For a long moment she continued to stare, and then turned the E-Meter around so that I could look at it. There it was, a small, folding box which opens up to stand on the desk in front of an auditor much the way a book would stand if you opened it in the middle and set it up like a small tent. A large meter faces the auditor, with a large dial on the upper left of the panel, a small on-off switch below it, and three knobs along the bottom: a sensitivity booster, a test-set-transit knob, and a trim knob. Two wires run out from either side of the whole thing and are clamped onto two tin cans. These cans are held by the *preclear*, in this instance me, and as the auditor asks various questions, some general, some more specific, the needle is carefully observed. And if it jumps. . . .

Hubbard once said: "The meter tells you what the preclear's mind is doing when the preclear is made to think of something. If they're emotionally disturbed about cats, and they're talking about cats, the needle flies about. If they're not disturbed about cats, the needle doesn't fly about. So you let them talk about cats until they're no longer disturbed about cats, and then the needle no longer flies about." It comes to rest because the disturbance is gone. Or because the battery inside the E-Meter has run down.

The E-Meter is actually a very simple device which measures electrical resistances. It is quite similar to the invention of Sir Charles Wheatstone—dubbed a Wheatstone bridge—on which the unknown resistance ( capacity to conduct electricity ) of an object or subject was measured by passing a very small charge of electricity through it and then comparing its conductivity with a known resistance. In Scientology's E-Meter, which was refined by Volney Mathison from the basic design of the Wheatstone bridge, a small battery provides the power to pass a very small charge through the leads and through your body. Scientology believes, according to a book called *The Hubbard Electrometer*, that the machine "measures the relative density of the body." What is measurable by the needle "is specifically the impingement of the individual himself (the spirit) upon the body by the direct action of thought." The current, Hubbard wrote in a handbook, *E-Meter Essentials*, "is influenced by the mental masses, pictures, circuits and machinery." As I examined the meter, I remembered the FDA case in Washington and the charges which followed. The E-Meter Miss Adler was showing me had that small message on it: "The E-Meter is not intended or effective for the diagnosis, treatment or prevention of any disease."

We were going to start with the Pinch Test, Miss Adler explained, and indicated I should pick up the two tin cans. She waited until I seemed to be holding them firmly, and then reached over to pinch my left forearm. She was wearing a very large orange stone ring on her left hand and I watched it, and as her hand got closer she watched the needle, and it sprang for the sky and she said, "Ahh. Anticipation." Yes ma'am. True. Anticipation. You're going to pinch me, lady. She had, by the way, made me take off my wedding ring, and I quickly figured out that its metal might impede or distort any reading on the meter. So she pinched me. Then she asked me to see if I could recreate the sensation. I screwed up my face a bit and summoned up my best Stanislavskian resources, and *I thought about that pinch*. I tried to make it happen again and found myself evaluating its quality instead. A good pinch. Decent. Well executed. The needle, meanwhile, was doing precious little. Miss Adler said "Good," several times. Which meant to me, Good, the needle isn't moving, or Good! the needle moved. It meant something either way.

Once that was over, she turned the E-Meter away from my view and said she would now do some simple auditing. I had put down the cans, which had gotten clammy in my fists. I picked them up again, quickly, wondering if she might be mad at me for dawdling. She looked at me. "What do you think of Scientology?"

"Well. . . ." What was I going to say? I liked it, I didn't like it, it frightened me, it didn't frighten me. . . . "I'm confused by it. There seem to be so many things to learn about it." I stopped.

Miss Adler saw I was finished and said, "Thank you," slowly, almost formally, and I realized the politesse was part of the procedure, integral to the consistency of demand and acknowledgment of answer. So she asked me again, just as naturally, her eyes dropping to the meter, which I couldn't see at all. "What do you think of Scientology?"

The cans were heavy in my hands and I did not want to start with another, "Well—" so I looked off to the side, as if thinking. Could she, I wondered, actually "know" how to read something from this rather simplistic machine?

The classic lie detector, or polygraph, had been developed in the crime detection laboratory at Northwestern University by Leonard Keeler, a one-time police officer from Berkeley, California. An article in the January 1967 *Scientific American* by Burke M. Smith, associate professor of neurology and psychiatry (clinical psychology) and chief clinical psychologist at the School of Medicine of the University of Virginia, describes the standard polygraph as "a simple, compact and often portable machine that records pulse rate, relative blood pressure, the rate and depth of breathing and often the resistance of the skin to the conduction of electricity" and makes the point that the machine is not specifically a "lie detector," but something which records physiological changes. "Any detecting of lies," he wrote, "is done by the examiner, the person who conducts the interrogation."

I felt Miss Adler watching me, waiting, so I said, still wondering about the efficacy of the E-Meter, "I think Scientology is *interesting.* . . . I want to know more about it, but I'm not sure what it has for me."

Miss Adler's eyes were now down on the meter and she said, "Thank you." And then she asked me the same question again: "What do you think of Scientology?"

"Nothing," I said evenly, taking the plunge, wondering if that might not be the *right* answer. (In his article, Dr. Smith had written: "The examining session is conducted in an atmosphere that is inevitably at least somewhat tense. . . .")

"Good," Miss Adler said just as evenly. "Thank you."

She went on to ask me the following questions, each two or three times, each acknowledged with a "Thank you."

"Do you have any problems with people?"

"Do you have any problems with your work?"

"Do you have any problems with the world at large?"

With that last one, after answering all the others humbly and with slight hesitations and mumblings, I allowed myself a small note of wry bitterness. I said, "Who doesn't these days?" It was obvious from all three questions that *anything* I might have felt the least bit worried about, concerned about, *guilty* about, would have eventually come out, if not then, then later, when I would be asked, in advanced auditing sessions, to be more specific.

After a final "Thank you," Miss Adler was finished. She fixed me with one of those eye-locks and asserted, very quietly, that I needed the HAS (Hubbard Apprentice Scientologist) Communications Course, that I put myself down a great deal and she saw that I could use the reinforcement of the Communications Course. I said I'd think about it.

The Communications Course is the first course of sessions you pay for. The cost can run from $15 to $25, depending upon where you take it, at the central organization offices or at one of the franchised offices. The Hubbard Association of Scientologists International, Ltd., only sets the base fees.

Before going any further into Scientology's techniques and exercises, I should describe the structure of your path on the route to Hubbard's Total Freedom. The Communications Course is the bottom rung of a ladder which leads into auditing and the first two levels: Straight Wire Release and Dianetic Release. Next comes Grade O Release, and then four more separate Grades, ending in Grade IV. The next step is to take what is called the DAC, the Dianetics Auditors Course. Its purpose is twofold, to introduce the importance of each individual functioning independently as an auditor, thereby suggesting that studying all the levels of professional auditing is much more valuable than merely being audited oneself, and to train one to audit oneself. After the DAC, one takes Grade V-VA, also known as *power*. This is followed by *solo*, Grade VI, and then Grade VII, *clear*, the temporal summit.

Scientology's activities are particularly confusing because at first glance there are no clear-cut lines visible between when one is expected to do one thing and when one might do another. To isolate them then: The buying and reading of the books provides Knowledge; attending and encouraging friends to attend the free lectures provides Orientation; the Scientology Congresses where one meets other Scientologists, shares experiences, and listens to tapes of L. Ron Hubbard lectures offers Enlightenment; the actual processing from one Grade up to the next is done to achieve Freedom; and the training courses through which one becomes an auditor offers Ability. The last, Academy Training, is made infinitely more attractive to prospective scientologists because it offers achieving *clear* for a total cost of $3,550, a savings on the $4,025 for achieving *clear* merely through processing. Elements of the Training Route, as it is often referred to, will be discussed later. To begin with, let me get into the Communications Course, where everyone really gets his start and where so many of the precepts inherent in Scientology's techniques are firmly established.

The experience of a young freelance photographer, Bud Lee, who was assigned to take some pictures of Scientology in action, dramatizes both what goes on in the course and how it is absorbed. Bud signed up for a $750 course which would have taken him all the way to Grade IV, and prepared himself for the Communications Course. The first lesson was called Confrontation, Bud explained, "where we were facing each other, with our hands on our knees, and we had to sit for an hour, without moving anything. Which is fine. I really believed in that. I could see the girl's corona around her, kind of a yellowish-green halo, and I thought this was great. I didn't know whether it was an optical illusion or what, but at least it was an experience."

As Bud told me about it, I couldn't help but remember Jack Kerouac's *On The Road,* when the wild poet, patterned after Allen Ginsberg, tells the book's narrator: "Dean and I are embarked on a tremendous season together. We're trying to communicate with absolute honesty and absolute completeness everything on our minds. We've had to take benzedrine. We sit on the bed, cross-legged, facing each other. I have finally taught Dean that he can do anything he wants, become mayor of Denver, marry a millionairess, or become the greatest poet since Rimbaud. But he keeps rushing out to see the midget auto races. . . ."

The second session of the Communications Course was called Bull-Baiting. Says Bud, "I sat across from my partner, this girl, and we were instructed to be either a coach or a student. In this case, she was the coach. And of course you're instructed to say anything; the Bull-Baiting is where they really break you down. Now the idea, you're supposed to overcome your subliminal mind and your body and you reach your optimum. When you've reached that, you've overcome all your prejudices, handicaps, your shortcomings in other words. The idea being that you can be happy, there's no need for any kind of neuroses. You can overcome a common cold, for example, just by reaching your optimum. So this exercise is the first of many where they're trying to break you. The instructress, whose name was Bobbie, or Barbara—she looked something like Bobbie Gentry: long black hair, a very, very good-looking body, but her eyes were very, very kind of hard, and she was always smiling and saying, 'Beautiful.' Every time someone made a comment in the class she'd say 'Beautiful,' or 'Groovy,' or give you a big smile. And she smoked, and was very, very relaxed. But very apart, not at all compassionate. Kind of a very withdrawn coolness about her. But very sharp. Well, the Bull-Baiting starts with—Bobbie had instructed all the students to sit in the same position as they sat in in the previous exercise, with your hands on your knees, upright, relaxed, and you're not allowed to move anything. If you move—like I have a tendency of dropping my shoulder—if they see something move, they yell, 'Flunk!' and then 'Start!' Your coach will tell you what you did. Well, the instructress started working on my bald head, and my pot belly." Bud is not bald. His hair is thinning and he is concerned about it and quite openly vulnerable to the notion that somebody would criticize him for that. He also does not have a pot belly. He is a large-framed person, with a kind young face, unexpected small lines of concern around his eyes, and a manner that is a trifle hesitant, but ultimately honest and quite unafraid. "She assumed I was a Madison Avenue ad account executive or something. She didn't think of me as anything else. And she looked at me and said, 'Your *affluent* belly,' and then, 'You go by that window every morning and you say, Maybe I should buy it, what would the boys in the office think? And then one day you bought some of this cream and you started working with this cream, and it said on the package that it would grow hair—' she started working on that. To me, she really wasn't that insulting because she really didn't get that far. She said that they don't call a cripple a cripple, or a black man a black man—there was this woman in the class who didn't have a chin, and obviously that point was made for her. And a lot of Negroes, a lot of different ethnic groups. So she said you work on other things, things that are not so obvious. The upshot was that I would laugh, and she explained that laughing is the emotion that is closest to the surface; you laugh before you cry."

Bud never took the last two sessions of the Communications Course. Later that evening, because he had been openly taking photographs, he was expelled and his money refunded. He was very upset, particularly because he was desperately interested to find out what was going to happen next.

What happens next is a session called "Dear Alice." It was described to me by Gary Watkins, the once highly placed Scientologist who was expelled by the movement for involving himself with a splinter group Hubbard felt was threatening him. The purpose of Dear Alice, Gary said, is "to increase your intention in communication, your ability to reach another person with exactly what you intended to reach them, rather than have your communication go off astray. It's done by reading out of a book, "Alice in Wonderland." You look down at the book and you look at the other person and you say: 'It's a Cheshire Cat.' Then you find another phrase in the book, and you go on." When done properly, Hubbard has said, the exercise increases "your 'ownership' of a communication. You look down at the book, you *own* that phrase, it's yours, you deliver it like it's yours." Says Gary Watkins, "People learn that book by heart before they're finished."

The next part of the exercise is something called Termination. "When somebody reads out of Dear Alice," Gary explained, "and says, 'It's a Cheshire Cat,' the other person says, 'Thank you.'" This is done "to increase your ability to acknowledge others, and acknowledge in a manner that means not just 'Thank you,' but End of Cycle. Completion of Communication. Over and Out. Or STOP. And very often that's what a Scientologist learns: 'Thank you. Stop.' Shut up. In Scientology, the thank-yous mean Completion of that cycle of Communication. Start a new cycle."

The final exercise in the Communications Course is one designed to increase ownership through "the ability to duplicate. Using Dear Alice, or some other text, one person reads off to another person, and that person has to tell them back specifically what they said. In all these exercises," Gary points out, "one is always in the auditor's position, or role, the other is the auditee."

At one time, the "termination" or "acknowledgment" drill was done using the E-Meter, to accustom students to the fact that something they say produces a "read" on the meter. Anyone taking the Training Route towards becoming a professional auditor would also take several TR's, Training Drills, which are not included in the usual Communications Course. TR's o through 2 are similar to the Confrontation, Bull-Baiting, and various uses of Dear Alice. TR 3 is called "duplicate question," meant "to duplicate without variation an auditing question, each time newly, in its own unit of time, not as a blur with other questions, and to acknowledge it." Asking such questions as "Do fish swim? Do birds fly?" students would do them again and again, for hours, striving to achieve repetition with no variations. In TR 4, a student auditor's coach would try to throw a student off by being difficult and not repeating "Do fish swim?" as directed. It becomes the student's task to make absolutely sure he can elicit a precise duplication each and every time, no matter what obstructions occur.

Once the Communications Course is over, you decide whether you want to take straight processing to achieve Freedom, or the Training Route to improve Ability as well as achieve Freedom. Anyone who decides to take straight processing begins with what is called Straight Wire Release, defined on Scientology's "Classification Gradation And Awareness Chart of Levels and Certificates" as achieving "Improvement in Memory and Ability to Recall." Before going into it, I have to emphasize a fundamental scientological principle basic to all processes and exercises. Hubbard described it in his book, *The Creation of Human Ability:* "The first goal which an Auditor much achieve is willingness in the preclear to receive directions. The condition of the preclear is such, in nearly all cases, that he has chosen as a main point of resistance in life, direction of himself other than his own." The result, Hubbard explains, is the continuous resistance on man's part to direction from the outside, which also weakens his ability to direct himself and, "it is the ability to direct himself which the Auditor is seeking to return to the preclear."

Every auditing session begins with a rigidly followed routine. The auditor must make sure that the preclear is comfortable in the particular room they are in. The auditor then says, "Start of session!" and they begin. In Straight Wire Release, three basic questions are asked: "Recall a communication. Recall something real. Recall an emotion." This continues as the preclear remembers various events or objects, gripping the cans until the moment his auditor tells him he has achieved Release, a needle which floats freely and no longer jumps on any of the answers given to those three questions: "Recall a communication. Recall something real. Recall an emotion."

The next level is called Dianetic Release and is designed, according to the chart, for "Erasure of Loss and Misemotion." The session consists of two questions, essentially: "Recall a loss. Recall a misemotion." This is certainly a far cry from the extensive auditing which was done during the Dianetics era with the auditee in *dianetic reverie*. Church of Scientology Minister Bob Thomas explained the more important differences in the new level of release. "Some of the early reverie technology that was used," he told me, "smacked a little bit of hypnosis, but certainly we don't use anything like that any more. It's not necessary. A person is fully aware, fully awake, fully alert, and no suggestions are made to him whatsoever. We start out in Dianetics by simply asking him to recall moments when he felt as though he liked somebody, moments when he felt he was experiencing something really real, moments when he felt he really understood something, things like this, which just kind of increases ability to recall. And then we go into a little bit deeper incident, and then a little bit deeper. But it's strictly a general question and command that's given to him, such as 'locate an incident.' And then we say, 'Okay, go to the beginning of it, move through it to the end, and tell me what's happening.' And that's it."

Grade O Communications Release gives one "Ability to communicate freely with anyone on any subject." Bob Thomas gave me an example of the type of question an auditor might ask. " 'If you could communicate to *blank*—whatever or whoever the person is having difficulty communicating to—put in that *blank*.' So he's having difficulty communicating with his wife; you'd say, 'If you could communicate to a *wife*, what would you talk about?' And then when we get a subject, we say, 'If you were talking to a wife about *that*, what would you say exactly?' Until the person feels much more at ease about communicating to that particular person or terminal, as we call it." Much more generally, this Grade is also run with two simple questions: "What are you willing to tell me about? What are you willing to tell me about it?" The most specific question anyone is ever asked during auditing, according to Thomas, is: "Should you have told me something you didn't?"

Grade I Release concerns Problems and acquiring the "Ability to recognize source of problems and make them vanish." The procedure is simply naming various problems and discussing possible solutions. The subjects covered can range from finances to sex to suicide to athlete's foot.

Grade II is Relief Release and involves achieving "Relief from hostilities and sufferings of life." The two areas dealt with on this grade are called "Overts" and "Withholds." The *Scientology Abridged Dictionary,* a copy of which every *preclear* is quick to purchase, defines an "Overt" as a "Harmful or contra-survival act . . . an act of commission or omission that harms the greater number of dynamics. . . . A failure to eradicate something or stop someone that would harm broadly would be an overt act." A "Withhold" is defined as an "undisclosed contra-survival act . . . in which the individual has done or been an accessory to doing something which is a transgression against some moral or ethical code. . . ." This Grade is achieved by answering two questions: "What have you done? What haven't you said?"

Grade III is called Freedom Release, "Freedom from the upsets of the past and ability to face the future." Scientology defines upsets as ARC breaks, breaks in the triangle of Affinity-Reality-Communications. The E-Meter is particularly important at this level because it is used to fix the date of any important ARC break. This is done by using what Scientology calls the "Over and Under" technique of asking questions pertaining to the sought-for date. The date is finally tracked down by process of elimination. When the incident has been properly fixed, it is rerun in detail until Release from it is achieved.

Grade IV is Ability Release, "Moving out of fixed conditions and gaining abilities to do new things." The general subject which is audited is something called "Service Facsimiles," defined as "an aberrated, non-survival solution the preclear uses to make others wrong, self right, to aid the survival of self, hinder the survival of others, help self dominate others and help escape domination." It is a combination of realizing when you have been passing the buck, as well as appreciating the intensity of your own determination to survive. The question asked is "What method have you used to make others wrong during your life?" Answers are written down, and with the aid of the E-Meter one particular incident is isolated and dissected in terms of its having been just such a "service facsimile."

All auditing sessions end the same way. A *preclear* is sent to a department known as Technical Services where somebody makes sure the *preclear* has truly ended the auditing session. This has been done by slowing down the pace of the questioning and initiating a careful reorientation to one's surroundings, bringing them back into "present time," sometimes accompanied with a demand from the auditor to have the *preclear* "Tell me I am no longer auditing you."

Achieving Grade IV in Scientology is known as having "done your Grades." Looking back on them, I remembered how Bob Thomas had broadly summarized what succeeding at each Grade level is meant to produce. "What we're really trying to do is increase the person's confidence in being able to remember what he wants to remember and not remember what he doesn't want to remember; increase his confidence in being able to control his memories. . . ."

It is at this point, after Grade IV Release, that you as a scientologist will decide whether or not to go into Scientology training. To continue up the ladder towards *clear* it is now necessary for you to take the Dianetics Auditors Course, which teaches the rudiments of auditing. Hubbard stresses the course's importance because in it, a person "learns the anatomy of the human mind, and gains practical experience in handling it in actual auditing sessions." The levels or Classes of Academy Training approximate the progress a *preclear* makes in his Grades, except that there is a somewhat different pattern of emphasis. You receive not only auditing, but "A Theory Course, with the appropriate certificate and a Practical Course with its levels of classification. The levels follow each other in a smooth gradient, and each level is properly mastered before the student progresses confidently to the next level." Local organizations can train you to Level IV, just as they can process somebody to Grade IV. Advanced levels and Grades are achieved, as was mentioned earlier, either at Saint Hill or at the new Los Angeles headquarters.

As I said, the essential difference between Academy Training and straight processing is initially one of intensity. As Gary Watkins described a person who takes the Training Route, "They'll take the Communications Course, but for weeks, the face-to-face stuff. Until they're letter perfect. They'll do one for one hour straight, and then another. Then they'll begin a process called 'Give me that hand,' a Havingness process, a Communications-Control-Havingness process." The drills in this group are called CCH's, and "Give me that hand" is CCH 1. "This," Gary went on to explain to me, "is definitely

an auditor-preclear situation, where the auditor and preclear
sit across from one another—the student in training is not
being audited, but the situation is exactly as it will be when
CCH 1 is used in actual auditing—and one person makes an
indication to their right hand and says, 'Give me that hand.'
They get the hand, they shake it, they acknowledge getting
it, say 'Thank you,' and then they place the hand back in the
lap. They'll do that for as long as it takes to 'flatten' it, meaning they have successfully done it three times without change."
To "flatten" is also an E-Meter needle term, but applies to
other facets of Scientology drilling as well. Gary continues:
"They're thus doing it under the auditor's control, based upon
the premise that the average person does not feel he is sufficiently in control of his life. By accepting the auditor's control,
he therefore somehow gets the idea that *he* could control
*himself* more.

"Then there is CCH 2, which is the auditor standing beside
the preclear, pointing to a wall, saying 'You look at that wall.'
Thank you. 'You walk over to the wall.' They walk over
together. He says, 'Thank you.' The preclear is supposed to
stop in front of the wall. 'Touch the wall.' 'Thank you.' 'Turn
around.' 'Thank you.' And you start again . . . until it's flat.
Everybody's pre-informed of what it's all going to be, and
what they're going to do. There are some absolutely wild,
fantastic things that happen to people during these exercises.
You would think it's a very simple procedure, but it is not.
Certainly on a repetitive basis it's not. Every psychotic tendency that you would imagine could come out of a person
when they're asked to do these things. Very few people come
in and do them cold. People will scream; everything comes
up: their resistance to authority, their objection to control,
their tendencies towards sickness, certain somatic illnesses or
pains they are not even aware of; because they are habitually
attempting to shut off their awareness, and suddenly they'll get
into better communication with their body and they'll scream,

and then they'll remember the specific incident relating to the pain.

"CCH 3 is 'Put your hand against mine.' You put your hands up. 'Follow and contribute to their motion—'" This CCH is also known as Hand Space Mimicry "—at which point you'll make a series of motions like this." Gary moves his hand around, the palm up, flat, as if someone's was being held against it, his movements decisive and varied. "First with your right hand and then with your left. It can be *beautiful* to do because ideally, perfect duplication and harmony with another person is a marvelous thing. If it's not overdone. And if a person is rational enough to appreciate what's happening. It brings a person's awareness and attention right, like that!" He snaps his fingers with a loud crack. "The rest of the CCH is: 'Put your hands one inch from mine. Thank you.' And you do the same thing. That's when it really is a groovy scene. That can be a ball. You do that up to a distance of three feet and after each time the preclear is asked: 'Did you contribute to their motion?' No matter what they say, you continue. Ideally, the answer is Yes, but it wouldn't matter; if they say No three times, it's flat. If they said 'No' three times the same way, without any significant change. It turns on automaticities: a person can start twitching, some people have eyeballs turn blood red and raw and then go back down again. A lot of things will turn up. This is a way, in Hubbard's language, of stimulating incidents, ailments, impulses, circuits, mental circuits, under control, that are stimulated by life out of control, and just wonk you, rather than you commanding the situation.

"CCH 4, you take a book—it's a silent process," also known as Book Mimicry, "and you say, 'I'm going to take this book and I want you to duplicate this motion.' And you do anything you want with it: hand it to them, etc., and that brings people's attention straight into present time, they're right with you. Some people can't do that. Their attention shoots out, because duplication is their factor, it's their out-factor and they're not good at it."

Looking at all of the CCH's, Gary says, "The first two are really 'turn-on' processes. They really bring up a lot of crap. Their purpose is to turn on, under control, those impulses or responses that life is ordinarily 'restimulating in you,' and therefore you experience it, observe it, key it out, to use his term, 'Key it out so it is no longer impinging upon you.' Under control. The second two will do that to some people to some degree but most often are present-time processes. Some people have trouble with CCH 3, but CCH 3 and 4 should be pure fun, you should be sailing right out of the muck you were in with CCH 1 and 2."

A person taking the Training Route will also learn something called Assists. There are two types. Physical Assists would be used if someone hurt something, like an arm. The student would learn to touch the area around the injury and say, at the same time, "Notice my fingers. Thank you. Notice my fingers. Thank you." And continue doing this around the injured area until it got better. The other type of assists involve someone coming in to a Scientology organization with a problem. An auditor would ask "Where was it? Thank you. When was it? Thank you. Who was involved? Thank you. What did the situation look like? Thank you." As Gary described it, "To get the person separated from that incident so that they're actually *looking* at the incident rather than being in it." This would be somewhat similar to the straight auditing technique used by a Class I Auditor to resolve general problems. Having asked "Do you have a present-time problem?" he would try to locate it and work it out according to what Hubbard labeled a situation's "intention," and its "counter-intention." As Gary put it, "What Hubbard really gets involved with in terms of problems and present-time problems he calls desensitizing problems."

To become a proficient auditor is not merely a question of

absorbing techniques. Says Minister Thomas, "It takes a great
deal of training. To be a highest level graduate auditor takes,
oh, probably between six months and a year of intensive
training. And by intensive training I mean full-time training,
as much as six to ten hours a day. It's comparable to several
years of college, I would say, in terms of hours."

As you as a student auditor progress up through the levels,
listening to lectures and taking courses and becoming first a
Hubbard Apprentice Scientologist, then a Hubbard Qualified
Scientologist, then a Hubbard Recognized Scientologist, then
a Hubbard Trained Scientologist, then a Hubbard Certified
Auditor, then a Hubbard Professional Auditor, then a Hubbard Advanced Auditor, then a Hubbard Validated Auditor,
then a Hubbard Senior Scientologist, and finally, at the same
time as achieving *clear,* a Hubbard Graduate Auditor, you
become more and more familiar with the many drills and
intricacies of operating the E-Meter.

The first few sessions involve simple familiarization, such
as simply touching the meter and then letting it go. You learn
all the knobs and controls, how to calibrate, how to set it up
on a table, how to squeeze the cans and thus how to direct a
future *preclear* to squeeze the cans, and how to read the tone
arm. A "read" on the meter is anything which shows up within
a tenth of a second of a question having been asked. As you
progress, you learn the various needle actions, each with a
different name: "Theta bop," "Rock slam," "Free needle,"
"Rocket read," "Tick," and others, such as "Stuck," "Null,"
"Speeded rise," "Slowed rise," and "Stop." To familiarize you
with reading the meter, a list called the "Preclear Origination
Sheet" is used. You hold the cans, watch the meter, and read
off this list which presumably duplicates most of the standard
responses you will hear from a *preclear.* "I have a pain in my
stomach." "WOW—I didn't know that before." "This processing
is worth the fee." "OUCH, OH OUCH." "Your eyes stink."
And about one hundred others.

You then learn what causes a "read" on a meter, and how

that "read" is "cleaned." "Cleaning" a read means locating its source. The exercise uses a particular passage from a book which creates a small "read," or "tick." The passage is reread until the one source of the "tick" is isolated and the "tick" itself is precisely duplicated.

Isolating dates is made more sophisticated in a drill called Track Dating. There are no set commands, but any date within hundreds of trillions of years can be set, beginning with round numbers such as "150 billion trillion years ago." This is located, using questions to indicate the "order of magnitude" of the date: seconds, minutes, days, years, tens of thousands of years . . . short of ad infinitum. "The last step of this drill," according to *The Book of E-Meter Drills,* which has been compiled by Mary Sue Hubbard, "the coach writes down a full date like this: *56,276,345,829,100 years ago, 315 days, 42 hours, 15 minutes, and 10 seconds.*" Using a "greater-than lesser-than" technique, you're supposed eventually to hit the date on the button.

You learn to differentiate "reads" of varying magnitudes by using prepared assessment lists on various subjects: "What is your favorite dog? Which tree do you like the best? Which fruit tastes the best?" etc., each question followed by a long list of fruits, trees, or dogs, each with its own "read." Gary Watkins explains applying this technique in actual auditing. "You found a goal by reading off a list of goals—the list is a list of lifetime goals prepared by that person—and you got a particular read on a goal. You found their goal, and their goal is to be a fish. So you've got this list and you say 'Who or What would want to be a fish?' because you want to find an Identity Terminal. A terminal or identity that they have assumed or borrowed from regularly in order to achieve that goal, or the identity they're trying to create all the time to achieve that goal. So you would say—you don't know which one it is—you say, 'Who or What would want to be a fish?' and you have a list." The person answers. "'Good. Who or What would want to be a fish?' 'A fish.' 'Good. Who or What would want to be a fish?' 'Well, a turtle.' 'Good. Who or What would want to be a fish?' 'Well, an octopus.' Fine. So you have this whole list, it's on this list somewhere, and it's got a particular kind of read. The right identity has what you call a Rocket Read that goes Pshoow! You read the question and the needles floating this way—" Gary holds a stiff palm up and then allows it the slightest, smooth undulation "—and 'Who or What would want to be a fish?' and they say, 'A turtle,' and Ptchui!" His hand swings down to one side like a lunging needle sucked to earth. "It takes off and then comes right back up." The point of the student using the assessment list is that he learns to know when that "read" has occurred. Such training can continue for many many hours. Says Gary, "You have to assess a list: 'Apples. Pears. Peaches. Sharks. Octopuses. Turtles,'—you're watching the meter while you're doing this. 'Apples. Peaches. Pears. . . .' You're not paying any attention to the person, couldn't care less, they're there as a convenience. You don't ignore them, but it's the 'reads' they produce which you're interested in." Where this process would be used would be at CLASS III, Auditing by List, what Gary calls "a very soft process."

But Auditing by List is important both in Academy Training and in Straight Processing. If you're receiving straight processing you may be asked, at almost any level, a general question such as: "Who might want to harm *blank?*" blank being an object, place, or person. And then you would be asked a list of a hundred items, each of which would match with something or someone who might want to harm that object, place, or person. The object which might be harmed is located, and then the "Who" of the question is located.

All of these drills and processes bring you closer to handling L. Ron Hubbard's predetermined concepts of what does or does not exist, with facility. *Power processing*, which is Grade V-VA, is based on mental manipulation of simple questions, as for example in the first part of Grade V, where one might be asked "What is no-source?" In the second part of V there would be two questions: "What exists?" "What have you done about it?" In Grade V-VA, you run names of people, and it can go on endlessly, as you, the *preclear*, locate a name which produces a "read" on the meter. The reason for the "read" is discovered and whatever "charge" there is on that name is flattened, as you are made to realize how you were victimized by the person in question, and how you victimized that person in return. If this appears somehow simplistic, you must remember that by Grade V-VA you know exactly what is being asked; Scientology has become a living language and the structure of existence as seen by Scientology is firmly established. To protect you from outside influences, when you take *power processes*, you wear a small tag pinned to your clothing: "I Am On Power Processes," it reads. "Please Do Not Ask Me Questions, Audit Me, or Discuss My Case With Me." The process itself can be run for fifteen minutes or fifteen days.

Grade VI, or *solo*, developed from Hubbard's theories about the existence of past goals, how they are implanted, and how we can free ourselves from their negative influences. Working in terms of goals, he evolved something called a Line Plot. On one side he wrote Terminal, which would represent what you wished to be. On the other side he wrote Opposition Terminal, which would be anything that might make it difficult for you to achieve your goal. This plotting looked something like this:

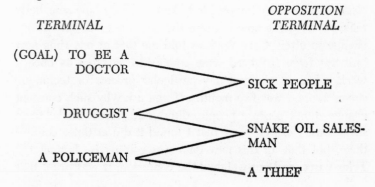

*TERMINAL*

*OPPOSITION TERMINAL*

(GOAL) TO BE A DOCTOR

SICK PEOPLE

DRUGGIST

SNAKE OIL SALES-MAN

A POLICEMAN

A THIEF

If your goal was to be a doctor, an opposition goal would be sick people—their existence would represent an opposition to becoming a doctor—and they, in turn, would be opposed by the existence of a druggist who might sell drugs which would cure them. The druggist, in turn, would be opposed by the snake oil salesman, who would be opposed by a policeman, who would be opposed by a thief. *Und so veiter.*

From this, Hubbard deduced that the accurate plotting must be done in terms of creation and destruction, based on his belief that in a cycle of action everything is an act of creation, and thus the creation of a negative was equal to the destruction of a positive, in other words, the negation of a negation. For the process itself, *solo,* you, the *preclear,* use a special E-Meter with a window in it so that you can look through it and see what you are writing and at the same time observe the needle and see when you have successfully "Blown Off" mass—the Mass of Goals-Problems-Mass. The Line Plot itself might look something like this as you work down it:

| TO CREATE | YOU DESTROY |
|---|---|
| UN-UNDERSTANDINGNESS | UNDERSTANDING |
| UN-INTELLIGENCENESS | INTELLIGENCE |

Once you have completed and been Released in Grade VI, *solo,* you are ready to go on to Grade VII, the achievement of *clear.* It is virtually impossible to know exactly how somebody makes *clear* right now because the techniques in Scientology change so often. Gary Watkins told me that at one time new bulletins from Hubbard were coming in as often as once a week, while the longest any particular process or technique stayed around was five months. If you ask why such constant change didn't confuse people, didn't and doesn't make them suspicious, I can only say that I found it did at times confuse them, but that all this new data was coming in, hot off the Telex wires, and out-weighed the confusion; it was proof that

L. Ron Hubbard—wherever he might be—was working away
to perfect every aspect of Scientology, purifying the techniques, making them better and better. As fas as going *clear*
is concerned, I know that you can make it either *solo* or with
an auditor; someone cleared recently on a list of twenty questions, being absolutely *clear* on every one of them. If the
definition of a Release is, as Gary put it, "being someone who
knows at this point that they're not going to get any worse in
life; they've reached a certain level of awareness and ability
and they'll never get worse," then a *clear* must be someone
who has achieved Release—I don't think it's wrong to use the
word Insight for Release—in every aspect of his MEST life.
My conclusions are that the *clear* processes themselves are
probably amalgamations of all the preceding techniques, taken
to the point where you can demonstrate not only control over
communications, over the source of problems, the achievement
of relief, the expression of Freedom, the knowing of Ability,
and the possession of Power, but the management of negations
as well, which is the beginning of those processes designed to
lead to something known as exteriorization—what we usually
call dissociation, a sense of total separation from your body.
The levels of these processes are called the O.T. Levels, the
grades of *operating thetans*.

Before I get into the O.T. Levels, I should digress to explain something which will help in understanding this concept
of exteriorization, as well as the notions of negating which are
so important to Scientology.

Hubbard had at one time called the structuring of the Line
Plot used in *solo*, R6EW, for Route 6 End Words. The Scientology dictionary defines this as words which create "locks,
words that are not in the GPM's but . . . are close in meaning
to significances that are part of the GPM's. They keep large
parts of the Reactive Mind in restimulation." Running this
process had at one time been the door to *clear:* Understanding—Nix-understanding; Communication—Nix-Communication.

Apparently John McMasters, the world's first *clear*, cleared on this very process, the negation of negations of negations, breaking through to envision the entire structure of existence precisely as L. Ron Hubbard had defined it, seeing this enormous, pomegranate-like mass, joined by bonds of agreements, a mass of goals held together within a person and forcing him to automatically negate reality without knowing what he was doing. R6EW was the process which unlocked those bonds and finally, by looking at both sides of the Graph—CREATE and DESTROY—demonstrating that only by negating a negation can one finally be *clear* and Totally Free.

The structured progression in Scientology processing and training only appeared in 1965. Before that there were various levels of attainment, but they were not codified to the extent of being defined as preceding one another in strict fashion. The reason for the structure was the discovery that running a person on a process designed for someone on a lower level was dangerous. Gary Watkins was one of the auditors who, as he explained, discovered "that if you had raised a person's ability and awareness to a certain point and then ran them on a lower level process, you did them in, and ran them back down." He found this out by working with a woman who, until 1958, had been extremely successful in business and in Scientology. She was being run on some of Hubbard's Creative Processes when her processing was changed. Says Gary, "Rather than running her on that, Hubbard abandoned that line of processing and some nut at some center ran her on a particular process called O.W.—General O.W., which means Overt Withhold: 'What have you done? What have you withheld?'—which that woman needed like a. . . . At any rate she was run on this for *weeks*. It drove her down, it started her on a downhill trend that ran until the winter of 1965." The woman began to drink, her marriage broke up, and she lost her job. Quite simply, she could not absorb the new insights and concepts she had been shifted onto, and it affected her much the same way a behavioral psychologist affects a rat in a maze when he wants to drive it crazy: he takes the existing "logic" of the rat's existence and replaces it with another "logic" or pattern or whatever you want to call it. Whatever it is, it is too much for the tortured animal to absorb, and it goes nuts. The woman, because she was a far more complex mechanism, did not quite go nuts, but she was damn close to it when Gary set out to discover what was wrong with her. "I said, 'Let's find out when the trouble started,' and we traced it back and we found it was in 1958. I notified the Org, and I said, 'This is critical!' They teletyped the information to Ron and it came out in a Bulletin two weeks later. And at that point he designed this chart—" the Gradation Chart "—saying nobody who had reached a certain level could be run at a lower level."

The Gradation Chart made its appearance in May of 1965. A few days later, in an HCO Policy Letter, Hubbard directed that "Persons who have attained Release may not thereafter be audited on any processes except Assists, By Passed Charge Assessments, Present Time Problems and Missed Withholds ['What have you done? What have you withheld?'] until they are trained up to Level VI and started on R6 processes. . . . The next action for a person who has attained Release is to take the next Course in Scientology and move on through to Clear properly. This is shown on the Gradation Chart. . . . There is no other way to Clear." The policy letter strikes me as being as close as Hubbard ever came to admitting that Scientology techniques advanced through nothing less than trial and error which, when you are dealing with people, is not the best way to reassure them that you always know what you are doing.

It took Gary a long time to locate the source of the woman's trouble. "She came," he recalls, "and I let her talk for a while. We cleaned up some things, some auditing errors that had been made. . . . There were specific ways to clean up auditing errors. There were two ways to do it. *Really* the way to do it is to get the person to start talking, and when they hit it, they'd know. And they'd get so upset, *you'd* know. That would be the main thing, you'd say to yourself, 'Yes, I've found the trouble.' And then say, to them, 'Could you tell me a little more about *that?*' At the same time, by watching the meter, you would know because it would start flying all over the place. Or it would get stuck. One or the other."

The woman had been run on an Exteriorization Process called Grand Tour, described in *The Creation of Human Ability*. It is defined as instructing the *preclear* to move to different points in space, to which Hubbard adds, "In the Grand Tour it is more important for the preclear to locate and occupy exact locations in space and in objects than it is for him to examine the surrounding areas." The woman, who had had no difficulty with the process, was being told to occupy several spaces, among them the top of the Empire State Building and the top of the George Washington Bridge. When she was taken off this process, she fell apart. Today, apparently free of Scientology, she is, according to Gary, "doing all right." More he could not tell me.

So that you don't think exteriorization is something like simply "imagining" yourself to be somewhere—the places the woman was told to occupy were chosen arbitrarily, it didn't matter where she was told to be—look at it this way: You physically occupy a particular place, and then you go "out of" yourself, knowing full well that you are still in your original place, and "be" elsewhere. It doesn't have to be far away. One girl told me, with an expression of small rapture, how she had come in to do Grade IV, and while she was doing it, suddenly "exteriorized." "I suddenly *saw* myself, the whole bit, sitting in that room. I was watching myself do Grade IV and I knew it was me there doing it." She shivered at this point, but it was a shiver of excitement. I mentioned before that exteriorization could be called dissociation, which is a splitting off of certain mental processes from the main body of consciousness. When you dissociate, you do *see* yourself as if from the outside. It is not just the power of suggestion.

Though the Creative Processes did not seem to work well with everyone, Hubbard was intrigued by their potential and never abandoned them completely. As Gary explained it to me, "Most people weren't up to it. He [Hubbard] found it was helpful to a point, but he couldn't stabilize a case at that level. He would help them up to fantastic levels of ability, but he had tremendous problems. He could not stabilize a case at the level he could help them achieve. People could create actions, and *do* things that were out of accord with their responsibility level." * The challenge was to raise the responsibility level. With time, as the Grades of Release were further developed, that responsibility level was achieved. In 1968, Hubbard announced what he called "100 Percent Gains Attainable by Standard Tech." Each and every process now works exactly as it is defined. The data used is stable. Everything works. The refinement and redefinition of the early Creative Processes had weeded out the failures, while the more esoteric techniques were now ready to be used. It is these which have now been restructured into the levels above *clear,* the Grades of *operating thetan.*

I do not know exactly what goes on above *clear.* The levels there are designated O.T. (*operating thetan*) levels, and there are eight of them, all available at a special 5 percent discount fee of $2,850. Scientology brochures explain that O.T. I is a step above *clear,* and in O.T. II "a being further expands, regains abilities and becomes ready for O.T. III." In O.T. III, "the student goes through the 'Wall of Fire' that no one could even approach without resultant sickness and death before L. Ron

---

* As an example, Gary suggested a brilliant salesman, silver-tongued and immensely persuasive, who can *sell* you a million dollars worth of goods, but then cannot deliver because he has not worked up to the million-dollar level in terms of stocking and supplying.

Hubbard found the way for you to go through safely and reach the other side, shining and free from the curtain of degradation that has hung like a poisonous veil over this planet." What Hubbard sees to be the "Wall of Fire," I don't know. I asked Gary Watkins if he could explain which abilities Hubbard would be perfecting at the O.T. levels. "They could be anything," he said. "Reading people's minds, communicating without verbal sounds, lifting objects at will, the ability to exteriorize and be at any point on the planet at your own decision, without negating your responsibility for having a body—if you ask me now I can tell you if it's raining in Washington—that type of thing." Gary rejected actually *doing* any of these things as cheap parlor tricks. When I pressed him on what a person would do with such super-abilities, he explained that it was suddenly realizing you *could* do them which was important, an explanation which coincides with Scientology's definition of the O.T. V Course: "Gradient scale drills to handle matter, energy, space and time from outside your body," and the O.T. VII Course where "one confronts at source the origination of thought and progresses up to realms wherein is revealed the total truths of spiritual existence and power."

Gary explained this more prosaically. "The ability to have full awareness in present time," is how he put it, "knowingly, so that you knew what was going on. You could walk into a room and be fully aware of eleven conversations at the same time and walk around and call people by name and contribute to the conversations at the right moment. A tremendous ability to command others, for worthwhile purposes, with affinity, in an enjoyable manner; have people do as you would have them do. Tremendous auditing ability in all counseling and perceptive abilities. The ability not to be subject, emotionally, to people who are victimizing themselves as a solution to life. Also, to destroy an object at will if you wanted." As to what processes are being used, Gary says, "If it is an extension of what I know they're doing to that point then it would be helping a person clear up their resistance to abilities which they have—" those abilities he mentioned before.

Once a person has become *clear* and has learned to negate negations, there are still, as Gary put it, "many areas of life which he doesn't want to confront and is unwilling to do." He is unwilling, at that point, to steal—the concept of eradicating resistances is something within his capacity, "but he does not like stealing in the actual world." Hubbard, at these levels, does not say there are things people dislike, he simply says that there "is something they *cannot* do. Then," Gary continues, explaining how Hubbard might structure the advanced techniques on the O.T. levels, "you have to raise your ability to confront What Is, and your willingness to be Cause over What Is, therefore get the idea of somebody stealing something therefore get the idea of stealing something. And the person says, 'Yes, I could have that command.' Boom! What else don't you like, what Effect in life would you be unwilling to be Cause over?"

Jack Horner defined it somewhat more specifically. "The Level VI materials—" the O.T. levels progress from I through VIII, "—leave a person in the position where he is pretty well in control of his own existence, his own life. One of the things about clear is that you realize you are surrounded by people still reacting to their own environment, who are not clear. There's not much game when you've got to play it alone. So the O.T. techniques go into the control and handling of the other dynamics." What Horner thinks they're using are the Route I exteriorization techniques from Hubbard's book *The Creation of Human Ability*, for example R1-4, which is "be three feet back of your head." Other processes in this Route direct the person to "mock up" things and then either destroy them or sustain them. By "mock up," Scientology means "a mental model, construction or picture created by a *thetan*."

One exteriorization process which is only whispered about,

but which everybody seems to know about, is called R2-.45, and is one of the 75 Route 2 processes also discussed in *The Creation of Human Ability*. No description accompanies its mention in the book. Only a small note: AN ENORMOUSLY EFFECTIVE PROCESS FOR EXTERIORIZATION BUT ITS USE IS FROWNED UPON BY THIS SOCIETY AT THIS TIME. What the process stands for, I was told, is R2-.45, the .45 being a .45 pistol. Hubbard is said to have marched out onto center stage at one of the Scientology congresses in Washington, D.C., in the late fifties, pulled out a .45 loaded with blanks, fired it into the audience, and announced to the stunned assemblage, "I just thought you'd like to see what R2-.45 looks like!" What no one is willing to say out loud is that this may be one of the advanced processes being taught somewhere at the present time.

# "ETHICS"

Scientology's theories and beliefs may be hard to take; the processes and techniques may unwittingly reveal something single-minded and pervasive about the direction of Scientology's drive; but it is in his reaction to derision, criticism, and attack from biased and unbiased outsiders that L. Ron Hubbard gives Scientology genuine dimension, an underlying quality which invisibly cloaks the whole phenomenal movement. It is Scientology's ethics which scare the hell out of me.

Hubbard has been getting it from all sides ever since the day he came out with Dianetics. He's not only used to it by now, but time has convinced him that you must use criticism and attacks to make yourself stronger. You face up to the adversity of ridicule and outside threats by pointing straight at them and challenging them to a sort of "anyplace, anytime" showdown. Hubbard instinctively knew he had to make something of each and every attack, exposing it to the cold light of Scientological reason, and use it to convince his brother Scientologists that someone somewhere was *afraid* of Scientology. There could be only one reason someone might be afraid of Scientology: They were afraid of the truth. In the late fifties, he wrote a pamphlet called "Why Some Fight Scientology," which was distributed to Scientology churches and organizations around the world. "Unfortunately," he wrote, "the person who does not want you to study Scientology is your enemy as well as ours. When he harangues against us to you as a 'cult,' a 'hoax,' as a very bad thing done by very bad people, he or she is only saying, 'Please, please, please don't try to find me out.' Thousands of such protesting people carefully investigated by us have been found to have unsavory pasts and sordid motives they did not dare (they felt) permit to come to light. . . ." Hubbard *never* identifies the protesters, massing them as a great unknown you know are there because he says they're there. It is an implied enemy, there because cold logic will tell you, even if you're the hardest-nosed scientologist of all, that there *must* be somebody out there against you!

Hubbard's polemic continues. " 'You had better leave Scientology alone!' is an instinctive defense, prompted in all cases investigated by a guilty conscience. Once they hear a few truths from Scientology such people become afraid. They *know* we know. And if we know this much and if you are further informed, they feel you will find them out. . . . Beware the person or group who fights Scientology, for that person fights Truth—not the truth of natural laws but the truth about himself."

At the same time that Hubbard was warning his minions against outside threats, he realized that Scientology was only as strong as its internal structure. His household security system, developed over the years, he calls "Ethics," and defines it as "reason and the contemplation of *optimum* survival." One of the first things Ethics tackled was to develop ways through which those individuals with unsure, vacillating, or even dangerous attitudes about Scientology could be unearthed, brought to the surface, and, if possible, straightened out, remedied, and helped. So Hubbard instituted security checks. When he first introduced them, they became an integral part of processing. An HCO Policy Letter of May 22, 1961, introduced "The Only Valid Security Check." It consisted of 150 questions, some of which were:

> Have you given your right name?
> Have you ever stolen anything; forged a signature, check or

document; blackmailed anybody; been blackmailed; cheated; smuggled anything; entered a country illegally, been in prison; tried to act normal; * indulged in drunkenness; done any reckless driving; hit and run with a car; burgled any place, embezzled money?

Have you ever assaulted anyone, practiced cannibalism, been in jail?

Have you ever raped anyone or been raped, been involved in an abortion, committed adultery, bigamy, practiced homosexuality, had intercourse with a member of your family, been sexually unfaithful, practiced sex with animals, practiced sodomy, slept with a member of a race of another color, committed culpable homicide, committed a justifiable crime, bombed anyone, murdered anyone, hidden a body, attempted suicide, caused a suicide, kidnapped anyone, aided an informer, betrayed anyone for money, threatened anyone with a firearm?

Are my questions embarrassing?

Do you have any bastards?

How could you help mankind?

What is Communism?

Do you know of any secret plans against Scientology?

Do you plan to steal a Scientology organization?

Are you upset about this security check?

What unkind thoughts have you had while doing this check?

What is important to understand at this point is not that Hubbard was convinced such a security check was beneficial, but that he firmly believed there were operating forces within Scientology which represented a specific danger. Thus, because his First Dynamic was to SURVIVE! it was only natural he take measures to insure that survival. The disgusting extremes to which he was willing to go were made clear in May of 1960, when he wrote a letter to Mrs. Penelope Elizabeth Williams, wife of Scientology's director for Australia and New

* I don't know if this question is designed to make sure that nobody escapes, or simply asks us to admit that at times, knowing we were not quite ourselves, we nevertheless, knowingly, tried to pass ourselves off as "normal." Talk about a Catch-22!

Zealand. In the letter, Hubbard revealed some damning discoveries about his associate and apparently faithful colleague, Jack Horner. "Horner," he wrote, "blew up in our faces and has had his certs. cancelled. We have criminal background on him. Rape of a girl pc in Dallas and countless others. This will do something to (_____). Now, I firmly believe you will be able to find a criminal background this life on (_____), as no such occurrence anywhere in the world has failed to find one. I'd grab him when he comes in and security check it into view." *Everybody*, Hubbard was positive, has something to hide.

After 1962, the security checks were no longer part of general processing and were only used for security purposes. A sense of necessary caution was already being felt, and a few people began dropping out of Scientology, concerned with the realization that somebody on the inside was actually watching them. At the same time, whisperings began about the only genuine palace revolt ever to shake Scientology. The extended adventure could not have been more timely. Hubbard responded to it with all the zeal of a latter-day Torquemada. It gave Scientology a very big plus as it struggled to expand as a spiritual movement deserving legitimate attention and fear because the revolt was nothing less than heresy. And every "religion" needs it.

It all began and developed with a man named Harry Thompson. Thompson had been one of England's most successful auditors, earning something approximating $20,000 a year, according to Gary Watkins. He was quick to absorb what Scientology believed and how these beliefs might be achieved, and easily ingratiated himself with Scientology through his genuine sincerity and expertise. Then, according to Gary, who now teaches Thompson's system in New York, Thompson "made a very simple discovery which aligned all the information in Scientology, as to why it was correct when it was correct, and why it worked when it did, and why it didn't when it didn't." Thompson went into retreat at his home outside London and spent three years developing and testing his discovery. He named it "Amprinistics," a combination of the words "amplify" and "principle." "What he discovered," Gary explains, "was Natural Law: Natural Law as a principle completely manifest in all universal activity from human behavior to the physical universe to social development." As Gary recounts the events which led to Harry Thompson's discovery, he makes sure he makes himself completely understood. It is almost a technique, a small residue from his dynamic days as a Scientology auditor. He stops to search for a word, and then resumes slowly, and as he sees he is on the right track, almost picks up speed and makes his point. His interests are now in Amprinistics, but he insists on a clearly defined attitude of decency when discussing Hubbard's response to Thompson's discovery and dissemination of Amprinistics. "I have a certain respect for Ron Hubbard," he explains. "I think he did some marvelous works. He's done a great job organizing a lot of information, of arriving at common denominators available in the knowledge of man. He made some tremendous advances just in the *idea* of what kind of individual progress a person could make." Gary is an extremely determined, fair-minded proponent of Amprinistics. About thirty years old, of short but muscular stature, he gives an impression of agility and physical poise. He has blond hair and blue eyes, and as he speaks, he cannot help but exude confidence, a confidence which almost throws him off stride, because he seeks *reason* and *understanding* rather than mere dynamic persuasion; he wants his listener to appreciate that there is a balanced view to be given L. Ron Hubbard and Harry Thompson and Amprinistics and the whole Ethics business.

Amprinistics was based on several basic premises: "The first," Gary says, "was that it is possible to discover the true nature of man and existence, that the answers are quantitative and available; that if you have true knowledge in regard to one aspect of existence or a man, it is interchangeable in that it will also be true for another man and another man and another man." Thus in Amprinistics, "the highest form of being, the highest activity, is purely knowing. The second highest— and this is in accordance with Scientology thinking—is action. Simply doing. Ideally, it would mean totally unhindered motion: Shooting through space without hindrances, action in its purest form of expression. And the third point on this scale, knowing, action, would be communicating about it." What Harry Thompson concluded was that there was a method by which to measure all phenomena: Identify it, handle it, and, through techniques, improve it. He sat down and wrote a letter about his discovery, and sent it to Scientologists everywhere. It was, according to several ex-Scientologists, "a beautiful letter."

Jack Horner was one of those who received it. This was late in 1964, and, as he explains it, he was "getting very uptight about the so-called Ethics." Horner had mended his several rifts with Hubbard and apparently had never even heard of the 1960 letter accusing him of rape in Dallas. "They," he says, referring to Scientology, "suddenly weren't answering certain letters. Not just mine, but certain people's. And I found that there was a policy that anyone who simply disagreed, their letters were called 'deadfile.' They weren't read, they just went into the wastebasket. About that time, Harry wrote me from England. He'd known me for about ten years. He said, 'Fly over to see me, I think I've got something I think is very good. And if it isn't, I'll pay your air fare.' I was so bugged by Scientology Ethics, the suppressive persons policy, I flew over to take a look." He saw that Thompson had organized his thinking into two basic areas of concepts: Primaries and Secondaries. Primaries, as Gary explained it, were "factual concepts that stand for real things that can be demonstrated." Secondaries, "have as their basis negations of primaries, or attempts to negate primaries." Thompson told Horner he had developed techniques which could be measured, and which demonstrated why they succeeded when they did, and why they were not applicable when not applicable.

Beyond the theories, there was a more fundamental difference between Amprinistics and Scientology, at least so far as Gary Watkins sees it. "Amprinistics," he says firmly, "believes everyone already knows and is in action. And because we do believe that, what we teach are improvement techniques. There are no mysteries, no religious aura." He interrupts himself, as if something just came to mind, and then says, all at once, "Hubbard's got a marvelous game, because the planet is clear now! So he says he's going to do it in ten years, you know, as if he's responsible for it. That's *not* his job. That's something every person lives with, himself, for himself: the degree to which he will admit and accept awareness." Getting back to Amprinistics, Gary says, in measured tones, "If you want to be crass, you could call us a service. Well, that's what we call ourselves, an educational service. We're straight out in the open: a profit-making business. And we're not going to hide behind titles, like religion, and so on. We pay taxes and all of that nonsense. We're in business to make money and we have a product. We have a product not only in terms of techniques and methods, we also have a product in terms of apparatus which assist in education. It's *all* strictly business."

It was early 1965 and Ron Hubbard knew there was something dangerous brewing within his organization. He had already introduced stringent methods to deal with anyone who represented any kind of a threat. He began to define various crimes which might be committed against Scientology, and labeled the types of persons who would be guilty. It was all absolutely classic, producing the most time-honored dissident known to man, the heretic. Only Scientology called him a "suppressive." This was any person who actively sought to suppress or damage Scientology or a Scientologist by *suppressive acts,* which Hubbard incisively defined as "actions or omissions undertaken knowingly to suppress, reduce or impede Scientology or Scientologists." Because Hubbard would certainly not settle for any half measures, the classic concept of guilt by association had to be introduced. This was the moment when a fellow Scientologist found himself branded a P.T.S. "Potential Trouble Source," clearly and cleverly defined as "any person, while active in Scientology or a preclear, [who] remains connected to a suppressive person or group."

Once Jack Horner had examined Harry Thompson's system, he liked what he saw, "and I wrote out a long letter saying that I thought that what Harry had was workable." And he sent it to Hubbard, which he now thinks might have been a mistake. *Might* seems an understatement. "His response," Horner told me, "was to declare me what is known as 'An Enemy.'" An HCO Bulletin went out naming Horner as having been relegated to the condition of "Enemy," to be considered "fair game," defined by Hubbard as somebody who "may be deprived of property or injured by any means by any Scientologist without any discipline of the Scientologist. May be tricked, sued, or lied to, or destroyed." Anyone associated with a "suppressed person" was immediately branded a Potential Trouble Source. I told Horner that being named "fair game," or relegated to a situation of "Enemy," sounded ominous. Had Scientology actually ever done anything to him? He hesitated, and then said, "I know that out in California, Chuck Berner's place—" Berner is a former Scientologist with his own movement "—they were shooting it up with guns. And about a week and a half ago I had somebody trying to kick in my back door with a .45."

"That's pretty wild," I said to him. "Assuming it might even be some infuriated, misguided Scientologist, don't the police take rather a dim view of somebody going around popping off a .45?"

Horner's only answer was a small chuckle, and I wasn't sure whether he really believed some Scientologist was after him, or maybe enjoyed the possibility that he, or Chuck Berner in California, represented such a clear threat to Hubbard that it could happen.

The only salvation for a Potential Trouble Source was to "disconnect"—remember the "renunciations" during the Middle Ages?—from whatever suppressive source he had been allied to. The "disconnection" could be from an organization, a family, or a single person, and had to be in the form of a letter, sent via the Ethics Officers, to the person from whom the disconnection was being made. Details of this procedure were outlined in HCO Policy Letters issued in March of 1965, and were followed up by HCO Policy Letters warning against Assist processing which ignored the need for Ethics control. In an HCO Policy Letter of August 9, 1965, Hubbard wrote: "Review Officer and Examiner please note, that if the person being Reviewed for whatever reason, has reads and/or answers on the part of the Review Form having to do with Ethics, HE OR SHE MUST BE SENT TO ETHICS, WHETHER THE QUESTION CLEARS OR NOT, AND WHETHER THE REVIEW ENDS IN A FLOATING NEEDLE OR NOT. Also, any Release of any stage who shows up in Review for an Assist is suspect of roller-coasting, so be alert. Roller-coasters are sent to Ethics." If a Scientologist has been away from Scientology for any length of time, for whatever reasons, he has to go through Review upon his return. "Roller-coasting" was Hubbard's definition of a person who gets better and then worse. "This occurs," he wrote, "only when he is connected to a suppressive person or group, and he must, in order to make his gains from Scientology permanent, either handle the source of suppression or disconnect from it."

Anyone sent to the Ethics Officer would have to answer some twenty questions directly connected to that question in his Assist or Review processing which produced the "read" found suspicious by either the Review Officer or the Examiner. When writer Alan J. Levy, deeply into Scientology processing as part of his research for an article he wrote for *Life* magazine, got a strong "read" involving his wife's name, he found himself answering a printed checklist of "potentially suppressive acts," which, Levy wrote, "my wife might have committed: Was she opening or with-holding my mail? Garbling phone messages? Listening in on phone calls? Denigrating my ambitions?"

The general tone of Hubbard's mood in 1965 was set more broadly by his HCO Policy Letter of August 15, 1965. It was entitled "THINGS THAT SHOULDN'T BE," and said, quite simply: "If you see something going on in the org that you don't like, and yet do not wish to turn in an Ethics chit, or indeed don't know who to report, WRITE A DESPATCH TO THE INSPECTION OFFICER. . . . The Inspection Officer will then investigate it and make a report to the right executives or turn in an Ethics chit on the offending persons himself." Thompson's letter was being passed around from hand to hand, and some people were beginning to ask questions.

In New York, an ardent young Scientologist named Jerry Tannenbaum also received a copy of the letter. Jerry, who now works with Monica Saxon, a former actress-dancer, teaching something called "Dramanatomy," the drama of the body, is of small stature, with fine features. The skin of his face is tanned a very light walnut and looks almost stretched over his bones. His long hair and loose-growing Vandyke beard make him look a little like a miniature Buffalo Bill Cody. He is slim-waisted and moves with light deliberation, suggesting someone who had once been tense, used to be physically on the alert, used to look quickly one way and then the other to see who or what was coming. Now, through the system Monica has developed over the years and which they teach together, he has disciplined himself to relax, and breathe, and live. "The letter was so beautifully constructed," he says, recalling Thompson's communication. "Things at that time had been getting a little tight in the organization, and I read it, and it just sounded so good; it merely stated that if what he had found was true, then you owe it to yourself to look at it, and if it isn't, it isn't. And Scientology had its Ethics thing, which said that if something were considered suppressive and you associated with it you would become 'suppressive,' but if you wrote a letter stating that you knew you now realized you were wrong, they'd take you back in. So I figured, well, I'll go look anyway and if it's wrong I can always write a letter saying I did absolute wrong. So I went and tried to present it to some Scientologists. It was incredible, the wall that started to build up between me and them. And it was so airtight, there was just no. . . . 'Hey man,' " Jerry cocks his head to one side, appealing to long-gone friends in Scientology, " 'this thing *just* says if it's true look at it, if it isn't, like, discard it. We're all supposedly looking for the truth.'

"Well, I had the letter, and I had shown it to some people in Scientology, and the Ethics Officer came down and said, 'What's this, about this letter you have?' I didn't know what to say. I said, 'I'd like you to read it.' It was really so beauti-fully constructed. She [the Ethics Officer] *flipped.* Words like: 'If this is true, Scientology will be forced to yield!' Well, she gave me the ultimatum after reading the letter that either I give this up, disconnect from that organization, or become sup-pressive. And I said, 'Well, I have to look at it.' And I did. Knowing that I could get back in by writing a letter."

Jerry liked what he found in Amprinistics and for a while he taught it. He had met Monica by this time and she allowed him to use her apartment for his sessions. Scientology, not content with declaring him a "suppressive," harassed him as well. "It was known that I was teaching the course in New York," he says. "The phone was ringing day and night. No-body'd answer. I have the feeling that they put Monica's name and number on a Men's Room wall because she got a lot of terrible calls from men."

At various periods during Scientology's history, L. Ron

Hubbard has issued amnesties. One of them, printed in an HCO Bulletin on his birthday, March 13, 1963, was typical. "On my birthday," Hubbard declared regally, "and on achieving my own fourth goal in clearing, and in celebration of the first Eight first goal Clears by 3M, I hereby extend and direct all the organizations, officials and staff of Scientology Organizations to grant all Dianeticists and Scientologists penalized before this date a complete amnesty. . . . Any and all offences of any kind before this date, discovered or undiscovered, are fully and completely forgiven. Directed at Saint Hill, on March the thirteen, 1964, in the 13th year of Dianetics and Scientology." It was not the first amnesty and has not been the last. Jerry Tannenbaum's reaction to them is bemused. "There have been amnesties before," he says, "and every time I'd gone in they'd tell me I had to do the same things I'd have to do if there wasn't an amnesty: I have to write a letter saying I'm completely wrong for what I did. Amprinistics is suppressive to Scientology. It's no good. It's dangerous."

When finally organized into some form, the Ethics appeared as a separate book, which, in a foreword, explained the purpose of Ethics as being "that additional tool necessary to make it possible to apply the technology of Scientology." The first part of the book introduced what Hubbard called the Anti-Social Personality, the Anti-Scientologist, among whose attributes is an inability to "respond to treatment or reform or psychotherapy." Hubbard polarized his discussion of this individual by next defining the Social Personality, and demonstrating how this type of person was basically well disposed towards Scientology. He then defined ten conditions, "operating states," ranging from a very top of Power to a very bottom of Enemy. Finally, he introduced the Ethics Codes, with its four classes of "crimes and offenses in Scientology . . . ERRORS, MISDEMEANORS, CRIMES AND HIGH CRIMES." Errors are classed as "minor unintentional omissions or mistakes," and are dealt with through self-correction "reprimand or warning." Misdemeanors, a bit more serious, could be either technical, general, or ethical, and, wrote Hubbard, "are subject to direct punishment by order." Someone on staff could find themselves demoted with their pay docked for a given period of time.

Crimes meant those acts "normally considered criminal," such as *non-compliance and neglect.* This was specifically defined as obeying orders or policies which were not legal and clearly not those promulgated by the International Board, and indulging in "alter-is," altering "the way something actually is" willfully.

Any incident of a staff scientologist accepting fees on his own was considered a *financial crime,* while a *technical crime* was committed when someone is or is turning-into a Potential Trouble Source and is not reported or acted upon. *General crimes* were getting a fellow staff member into trouble by lying. So were "heckling" and "mayhem."

Punishment for these crimes is meted out by courts of ethics or committees of evidence. Not directly. Guilty parties may find themselves with suspended certificates, classifications or awards, demotions, or may even be thrown out of Scientology. And if the crime calls for it, the criminal can also be arrested.

At the very top, the most serious, are the *high crimes (suppressive acts),* which includes "Attacks on Scientology and Scientologists, Disavowal, Splintering, Divergence, Technical High Crimes" such as "tolerating or not insisting upon star-rated checkouts [*Star-rated checkouts:* Technical or administrative material of highest importance checked on the person studying it by another to make *sure* the person knows and can apply it exactly] on all processes and their immediate technology and on relevant policy letters . . ." and the "CRIMINAL ISSUE OF MATERIALS."

Hubbard does say that "the right to petition must not be denied," but directs that "Collective petition is a crime under Ethics as it is an effort to hide the actual petitioner and as there may be no punishment for a petition, collective petition has therefore no excuse of safety and is to be interpreted as an effort to overwhelm and may not be regarded as a petition." *Introduction To Scientology Ethics* ends with a brief chapter called "Rewards and Penalties," a discussion of social histories as assessed by Hubbard on the basis of their survival when the citizenry was properly rewarded, and collapse when such reward was denied. Discussing what he believes to be the real cause of the Depression, Hubbard appears to be arguing for a rewards system which will convince Scientologists that his Ethics system serves only to penalize what he calls a "down statistic" that genuine success in Scientology will always be rewarded.

Hubbard has allowed himself the trouble of defending the harshness of his measures, particularly the designation of someone having committed a High Crime as "Enemy," by writing, "Now get this as a technical fact, not a hopeful idea: Every time we have investigated the background of a critic of Scientology, we have found crimes for which that person or group could be imprisoned under existing law. We do not find critics of Scientology who do not have criminal pasts. Over and over we prove this. Politician A stands up on his hind legs in a Parliament and brays for a condemnation of Scientology. When we look him over, we find crimes, embezzled funds, moral lapses, a thirst for young boys, sordid stuff. Wife B howls at her husband for attending a Scientology group. We look her up, and find that she had a baby he didn't know about."

As regards organizations such as the people in Amprinistics, Hubbard wrote: "They are declared enemies of mankind, the planet, and all life. They are fair game. No amnesty may ever cover them. The Criminals Prosecution Bureau is to find any and all crimes in their pasts, and have them brought to court and imprisoned."

I asked Church of Scientology Minister Bob Thomas what

he thought of Amprinistics, and he, with characteristic sobriety and calm, said, "Scientology took a dim view of them because they had altered the technology and made it into a personalized and non-Scientological application for which they were expelled from Scientology. If you have a *cancer*," he said with simple directness, "you cut it out."

"We insist," he went on to explain, his manner so incredibly *mild* and forgiving, "on a standardized application of technology. Anyone who alters it, of course, is not practicing Scientology as we have standardized it. Organization and standardization of the technology is required to have a mass movement for freedom. There's no contradiction." As for the people like Gary Watkins and Jack Horner who have been expelled, Thomas says, "it isn't like excommunication. It's a modified excommunication because they can come back in."

Jack Horner doesn't take such a benign stand. "There are several thousand people right here in this country who basically go along with the techniques and the processes and the applications of Scientology and its philosophy. But they will not or cannot, for whatever reasons, go along with the Ethics." What I cannot reconcile in my mind is the almost burning desire on the part of these thousands—I know they exist—to even try to come to any kind of terms with a man and a system which invented and developed and practiced this cruel gestapo-like security system.

With its policies of "suppressives" and Potential Trouble Sources, Scientology was not only busy cutting out people inside the organization, but was reaching out to try and choke off any outsiders who appeared in any way dangerous. Ray Buckingham, an English-born voice teacher and artist's representative in New York, first learned about Scientology when one of his students, a girl named Mary Vonnie, went to Scientology for help. According to Buckingham's testimony at the Scientology tax hearings in Washington, D.C., Miss Vonnie had some serious personal problems when she first came to study with him. Scientology appeared to help her and she involved herself seriously and after six months of training in Washington, D.C., became a full-fledged auditor. She discussed Scientology with Buckingham, who expressed more than casual interest. He bought several of the books and eventually took some processing from her, in exchange for voice lessons. All this stopped when he discovered that some of the information he had told her was being passed on to the Founding Church in New York. Buckingham felt this to be clearly unethical, and said so. He had, in the meantime, urged several of his other pupils to try Scientology. Shortly after he was no longer being audited, he began to hear some rather strange reports about himself, including one from a talented young musical comedy singer and dancer, Julie Migines, who told him one day, as he related at the hearings, " 'I was audited today and I just learned that you killed me in the last fifteen lives.' "

At the same time that all this began to happen, Buckingham's fiancée was becoming deeply involved with Scientology and was being slowly estranged from him by, as he described him, one of Scientology's "doctors of divinity." His fiancée was made to disconnect from him and told him he would die shortly because he was a Potential Trouble Source. When Buckingham finally went to the offices of The Founding Church of Scientology and spoke with one of the Ethics Officers, he was told that his problems stemmed from his association with a man named Carl Eugster, a colleague, and a collaborator with Buckingham in a business venture, who was a "suppressive." Only disconnection from Eugster could allow Buckingham to clear up his personal affairs. When he demanded to know why Eugster had been declared "suppressive," he was told that it was all because Eugster, in turn, had been associated with someone who was a "suppressive."

In 1966, Ray Buckingham went on a local New York radio program and discussed what had happened to him. Scientology immediately issued an official declaration of suppression. In an HCO Ethics Order dated November 22, 1966, he was accused of public disavowal of Scientology, threatening to attack Scientology in Civil Court, causing disconnections and concern to former pupils, refusing to disconnect from Carl Eugster, and "DECLARED also in the same radio program—that a 'True Philosophy' would not charge for its service—thus denying any 'True Philosophy' the right to survive in the physical universe." Buckingham was not to be communicated with by any Scientologists, was never to be trained or processed, and was declared "fair game." "PERSONS CONNECTED with him are hereby Declared POTENTIAL TROUBLE SOURCES and are not to be trained or processed until they HANDLE OR DISCONNECT: or themselves be Declared SUPPRESSIVE if they refuse or do not accomplish it within a period of three weeks from this date." The order was signed on behalf of L. Ron Hubbard by the New York Ethics Officer.

At much the same time, Carl Eugster, Buckingham's supposed "suppressive" connection, found his wife and son declared Suppressives because of their refusal to disconnect from him.

As a result of the Suppressive Order against him, several of Buckingham's clients disconnnected from him, each writing a letter which was approved, and in some cases initialed, by the Ethics Officer before being sent. "It may interest you to know," Mary Vonnie wrote in her letter, "that the effects you have caused have not and could not ever injure Scientology and the achievement of its purposes, but if one or two people, not quite objective enough to see what's in front of them, should become blinded by the bank you restimulate on them, then one or two people have been delayed on the road to Total Freedom. This is the greatest effect you can cause. Heavy restimulation of a few people who also feel that they must be punished." The letter closed with a decisive "That's it!" and her signature. Another, not quite as direct, began on a note of sadly accepted sorrow: "I had hoped that during

[the] three week period after you made yourself a suppressive towards Scientology, that I would be influential enough to get you to take steps to change that condition." Reconciling to a failure to achieve this, the letter writer went on to express admiration for Buckingham's teaching abilities, adding "It seems to me that this is the only area in which you do not commit overts and that's why this area is so prosperous for you." The letter closes with a last energetic plea. "Gosh, Ray, I don't have to tell you a thing. If you could only hold off your Bank while thinking about this Ethics bit, you would see that Ethics is right." The letter was signed, "Sincerely."

The shortest disconnect letter I have seen came right to the point and was unavoidably poignant. "Dear Ann," it read, "I hereby disconnect from you. Love, Barbara."

It is hard to absorb exactly what Scientology Ethics has in mind when it orders that "suppressives," or those designated as "Enemy," should be punished, or that they can liberate themselves from their condition by punishing the agent of their suppression. Jerry Tannenbaum called up the Church of Scientology one day not too long ago to talk to an old friend. "I called up," he says, "to get a receipt for some land I bought from him. I gave my professional name, otherwise I wouldn't have gotten through. And I said, 'Hi, Milt. This is Jerry. I'd like to get—' And he just cut me off and said: 'The terminal you want is Ethics.' I said, 'Milt, I just want to—' 'The terminal you want is Ethics!' Then Ethics—it was crazy—this girl, a young girl, and *she* was taking care of Scientology Ethics. She said, 'Are you still in Amprinistics?' I said, 'Listen, I was out of Amprinistics about two and a half years ago. There isn't even an organization here, except what Gary started, and this was before he started it. I don't communicate with the guy or anything.' And she said, 'Well, it still exists and until it no longer exists on this planet, until you do something about it. . . .' I said, 'Huh?' And she said something about I should help 'kill it.' I thought, Whew! that's a *beautiful* way to talk over the phone."

Because of increased public attention and more and more criticism regarding the Ethics policies, Scientology has found it necessary to make what it feels are important public accommodations. In the Public Notices of *The New York Times* in November of 1968 the following announcement appeared: "The Church of Scientology wishes to make known that the policy known as disconnection is now ended. One individual no longer needs to separate from another. A policy dated November 13, 1968 states 'since we can now handle all types of cases, disconnection as a condition is cancelled.'" Early in January, English Scientologists delivered six boxes of unused security checks to the Department of Health and Social Services as a dramatic gesture to show that the checks were no longer in use. A representative of Scientology, David Gaiman, was quoted as saying: "We have made a very honest and expensive attempt to find out what we were doing that was unacceptable by the community, and we have brought out a code of reform." Later that month, the following was circulated in Scientology's various magazines and newsletters:

AS THE RESULT OF ANSWERS TO A QUESTIONNAIRE CIRCULATED WIDELY IN VARIOUS PARTS OF THE WORLD, THE CHURCH OF SCIENTOLOGY HAS EVOLVED THE FOLLOWING CODE OF REFORM TO BRING ITS POLICIES MORE IN LINE WITH THE NEEDS OF THE PUBLIC:

1. Cancellation of disconnection as a relief to those suffering from familial suppression.
2. Cancellation of security checks as a form of confession.
3. Prohibition of any confessional materials being written down.
4. Cancellation of declaring people Fair Game.

As much out of curiosity as anything else, Jerry Tannenbaum heard about these latest changes and immediately went down to The Founding Church of Scientology. He spoke to the

Ethics Officer, wanting to know how one now went about getting reinstated. The Ethics Officer gave him a copy of the HCO Policy Letter of 6 October, 1967. It was a printed definition of the "Condition of Liability," the "Condition of Treason, The Condition of Doubt, and the Condition of Enemy." Under Liability, one of the requirements was to "deliver an effective blow to the enemies of the group one has been pretending to be part of despite personal danger." Under Treason, one of the conditions was to "Perform a self-damaging act that furthers the purposes or objectives of the group one has betrayed [Scientology]." Under the Condition of Enemy, the formulas had been crossed out and a single one inserted: "Find out *who* you really are."

As Jerry said, "I told the guy, 'hasn't there been an Amnesty?' and the guy said, 'Here's what you have to do.'" Jerry smiled, still mildly surprised by his own personal sense of amusement at the brief confrontation, and added, "It hasn't changed at all."

# THREE

# CONCLUSIONS

Early in this book I wrote that I prefer complexity in man; a search for simplistic formulae not only offends me, but frightens me. I have to add that I loathe anything which preys upon human weaknesses. I know you can broaden this statement so that it includes every organized movement of faith ever known to man, but Scientology has been so shameless, so blatantly vulgar and, yes, commercial, in telling its adherents all about The Truth and how to achieve it, that it has made a unique place for itself in our times. The facts speak for themselves eloquently.

I

Somewhere in all the millions of words written and spoken about Scientology, L. Ron Hubbard manages to tell us exactly what Scientology's intentions and goals are and how it plans to achieve them. The various processes and drills may be hidden from casual outside view because of Scientology's ultra-strict code of internal ethics, but the entire phenomenon of this mass movement was never more clearly and honestly defined than when Church of Scientology Minister Bob Thomas told me that Scientology strives to help a person *control* his memories. While this may go far in explaining the processes and drills, it throws little light on some of Scientology's more fanciful theories and beliefs, and does little to explain *why* so many people are getting into it. Some clue to the latter may lie in the types of persons drawn to Scientology.

Jack Horner put it this way, when he said, about himself and the majority of those who involved themselves with Scientology in the early days: "Most of us were reasonably pragmatic, heuristic, if you will. It was a question of does this bring about beneficial changes in people, and if so, good." Horner added, quite candidly, "We weren't in Scientology for games— we *were* in a way—but the point is that we were quite serious about it. For a lot of us in Scientology, while it might have had parts of it that weren't right, it was the only game in town."

Jerry Tannenbaum's view is broader, and gentler. "There are so many ways I have looked at Scientology," he told me, "in terms of its existence at this time; whether its existence is in actual fact good or bad. And when I view it that way, I couldn't say it's either good or bad. I could say, based on studies of other philosophies, Eastern philosophies, that a person is attracted to it if that's his Karma; if it's his Karma to be stuck in it and to be mentally hurt. That was the design, it's already in the cards for him to have that experience. When you talk about it in terms of Western philosophies, and psychology, it's very destructive. It makes an automaton out of a person. It robs that person of his own individuality. But these expressions are Western philosophy expressions."

Looking back on his own life, Jerry, who now embraces the tenets of Tibetan Buddhism, said, "I was naïve, because I hadn't studied anything else. I studied sociology and psychology at college, then went to the Summerhill movement. I dropped out of college. I was . . . like that educational thing bothered me very much. There was not much that could be accomplished there in a short period of time. And I was energetic in that sense. After Summerhill I heard about Scientology and I met some people that were in it. They told me about it and it sounded great. It was the first time I heard of past life and actually studying it, so I was taken right in, and I really went in hook, line and sinker, and I was very, very dedicated—that's a horrible word, *dedicated,* 'cause it starts with *ded*—and I was a great Scientologist. I had a lot of very warm friendships. There's one thing about the people all working together like that, as Hesse said in one book, *Demian,* when he saw all the soldiers going towards the front: he said there was something magnificent about the movement, their desire to move, to get the enemy. The shame is that they're so willing to die for a cause, instead of living for one. So the people in Scientology were like that, giving of themselves with tremendous energy for what they believe was good, which . . . it's a beautiful feeling." He paused for a moment, obviously remembering how it had all come to an end. "It was a little shocking when I left," he said with understatement. "All these friendships were just, Bluuunkk!" and he wiped his hand through the air as if erasing something with one broad stroke.

When I asked Gary Watkins what he thought the biggest thing wrong with Scientology was, he sat back to think, then hunched forward, rested his elbows on his desk, clenched his hands, and then laughed, to himself, and thought some more. It was a long time before he spoke. "The basic objective of the entire field is based upon the premise of clear, that people are unenlightened. The thing with Scientology is you first have to convince a man that he's not clear, and then tell him you'll clear him." Why, I wondered, was it made to look so complicated and inaccessible? Because, Gary said, "Ron Hubbard's understanding of problems people have, and his general understanding, is in terms of extraordinary phenomena. The books and the charts, they tend to complicate matters rather than simplify them. He didn't give enough credit to people: where they were, and what they do know and what they are accomplishing. It's a convincing story, it's really a convincing story. I would say, maybe, if Ron Hubbard hadn't gone through all this, somebody else might've had to, eventually, to go through all the complications. He made discoveries that were well in advance of discoveries made in psychology and psychiatry, of aspects of mind, aspects of behavior, that eventually somebody would have come around to. The business of psychosomatic ailments being 70 percent of all ailments; a little bolder than anyone else, but psychologists and psychiatrists *admit* such phenomena." But there was always a personal quality to Scientology, L. Ron Hubbard's presence, and wrath, and it gives a cautiously realistic tone to what Gary says next. "Every time anybody got very close to it [Total Freedom], he stopped them. Every time anyone created successful promotion, he kicked them out, pulled them out of a post. Every time anyone started to gather a reasonable following, he shipped them out, or changed their function."

Putting all this together rang a small bell, something Jack Horner had said which I felt was on a lot of people's minds. "If I thought," he had said, "there was any way of working with Ron, I would, but I don't see any way of doing it." This one thought, common to so many ex-Scientologists, nagging them as they discuss their personal experiences and wonder about the philosophy and the man who made it all happen: What if he is right? What if, despite those personal qualities of Hubbard's which are dubious, despite that shattering moment when Scientology turned on them savagely and threw them out, despite their own analyses which reveal disparities and loopholes: what if L. Ron Hubbard really grabbed something big and worked out a system which does give you all the powers he identified, and what if his is the first and only system which can do it? It is frankly a terrifying thought.

But if it is right, and if that door to Total Freedom is exactly where Hubbard said man will find it, why all the fancy lingo, and the almost intentional intricacy of the gradients, as if it is more important to keep climbing up that ladder than reaching the top; as if L. Ron Hubbard—and it is a suggestion which crossed my mind often as I talked and read and wondered about Scientology—himself doesn't know where he is going. That what is important is just to keep it all *going*. Somewhere.

Bob Thomas, who is now head of the Hubbard organization in Los Angeles, and has become probably the most important Scientologist in the United States, explains this seeming contradiction calmly. "As the research advances the technology changes at the advanced level. It doesn't confuse, because the lower levels are not changed very radically by any of the new researches. It's like every stage of development that's reached, the next stage is researched and then put out." Doesn't that, I asked him, make processing eternal or endless? "If processing is eternal," he answered, "it's only because the degree of rehabilitation of the human being, from our point of view, is eternal. But there are finite states of attainment, approaching this infinitude. We have no limitations, we project no limitations as to how powerful and advanced a state of consciousness man can attain." What I really felt, I said, was that Scientology seemed enveloping, always there, to be lived with every moment of every day. Thomas disagreed. "Let's face it," he said with candor. "Everyone has a philosophy of life, whether they have articulated it or not. It's with them, in terms of the structure of their viewpoint. How they would verbalize it varies, but they all have, basically, some assumptions about life which are with them always." When I suggested that it all seemed as if man might never be free, totally, because he would always have to depend upon Scientology to show him The Way, Thomas said, "Freedom is a relative term. One of the basic Scientology viewpoints is that absolutes are not attainable in the physical universe. But you can get more and more and more free, and that's what's happening in Scientology: people are finding out more and more about themselves and the more they find out about themselves, the freer they are. We envision no ultimate limitation on how free an individual can be. The researches that Mr. Hubbard is doing are designed to carry man forward toward that ultimate goal of Total Freedom."

More than one person has wondered about these current researches of Hubbard's, and his research techniques in general. During its investigation into Scientology, the Board of Inquiry in the state of Victoria, in Australia, heard one witness testify: "We never saw Ron actually engaged in research . . . because, as I understand, a lot of research was done in the early hours of the morning, but . . . the fact that the course was going, [that] was also part of the research program, as he would observe students and see what they were doing, and then, in his own time, what was going wrong and correct it. . . ."

Another witness stated that "sometimes Ron would say if he wanted to do research on a certain process and there was at one time a number of students selected to run this process, but the majority of research he gets Mary Sue to run. So whatever he worked out, Mary Sue runs on him before he uses it."

Nick Robinson, the young Englishman who had spent enough time on board Hubbard's flagship to observe the man at work, said, "The way Hubbard did his research, so far as we could see, was to scout around the islands and the coastline of the Mediterranean and see what it suggested to him, you see. He was supposed to have total recall of past lives . . ." and "one incident which he described at the party following his return was that he had docked at Sardinia, and two thousand years ago, according to him, he had been the commander of a fleet of war galleys in the Mediterranean, and he had had an affair with the priestess of the Temple of Sardinia, and he used to make assignations with her by her secret tunnel into the temple—it was all beautiful Rider Haggard stuff. Well, at the island he made a little plasticene model of the secret entrance and sent his troops around to scout around for it. And there it was, lo and behold! It was a stone which resembled the model. They thought this was the entrance. And when Hubbard described this at the party celebrating his return—" arriving at this exact spot two thousand years after the fact to find a large stone he had duplicated in clay, "the whole room sort of erupted into crys of 'Good Old Ron!' and whistles. I think I was the only one there who thought, 'Well, this is marvelous showmanship, but it doesn't prove a damn thing about past lives.'"

Monica Saxon, who developed the techniques of Dramanatomy which Jerry Tannenbaum teaches with her, looks back on Scientology with an insight which preceded her involvement. "I didn't go into Scientology to become an auditor," she says. "It looked interesting, and I went in to look at it. I was in classes where people audited each other, and with private auditors, and I reached clear—what they were calling clear then." There is a controlled serenity about Monica which comes through in her well-modulated voice; there is an unwillingness to laugh easily, yet a smile, when it comes, is warm and sincere. She has an oval, high-cheeked face, and eyes that are wide and soft. Her hair is long and falls down her back, and when she moves, you can see her full stature and the ease with which she gestures or takes a step. It is almost a dancer's body, implying great strength and control. Her eyes watch and listen and she answers directly, with objective self-knowledge. Her disenchantment with Scientology began at a congress in Washington, D.C. "The whole presentation," she explains, "was like a snake medicine show. He [Hubbard] even had a drummer, who would drum—" she rises and takes a determined pose, her right arm raised above an imaginary drum, "—as he was walking around, to make a point in his speech." She strides across the floor, her step purposeful, majestic. Then she becomes the drummer and lifts her arm, and then drops it. "Boom! and he would go into his point." She stops and turns to look at me. "Like indoctrination. Brainwashing. You know who he reminded me of? He looked like a cross between Wallace Beery and W.C. Fields; W.C. Fields in those movies being a snake-oil salesman. Even his delivery was of that nature. And I'd been in show business for years before I did this work, and I looked, and I thought, Wow! this is a Big Show. I met him personally during the Congress, and he was playing the Great God. Just the way he'd say, 'How do you do—'" Monica's look grows almost somber, ministerial, her hand-clasp solid and cool. "He was presenting himself to be worshipped, really."

Yet some of the processes in Scientology genuinely appealed to her. "To look at Changes," she says. "If I was the auditor and you were the preclear, I'd say: 'Get the idea of changing.' And then you'd say something back to me, or just, 'Yes, I got the idea.' And then I'd say 'Get the idea of not changing.' And then you'd look at that and either say your idea of not changing or else just say, 'Okay, I got the idea.' This would be repeated for one hour. And then at the end of the hour we'd change and you'd become the auditor and I'd be the preclear and you'd give it to me. I found that was very creative; I looked at my own mind, how my own mind worked with the idea of changing or not changing, and that, to me, was what I was doing with that process. I don't know if anyone else was doing that with it."

Her criticism of Scientology is very simple. "What I really feel is that the whole technique—what he uses as technique—is training people how to indoctrinate other people. There's that certain point that you reach when you have to go through training to be an auditor to go beyond that. Actually, what happens with the training, what I saw, it's pretty strong: you get indoctrinated and pretty soon you—I watched the people, what they were doing before just slips away. And suddenly they're all *auditors*. It's drummed at you and drummed at you, and the memorization, what they call 'duplicating the data,' the memorization is strong so that there's no room—it pushes— it's like taking something and pushing it into a person at such speed that anything that they had before is pushed right out. You come out a scientologist."

Monica left it all in 1962. "When I was doing these processes," she says, "there wasn't any Grading going on with those particular types of processes. When they began to Grade, that's when I left. Because I felt, I am the judge of whether I got out of *that* what I wanted, and for someone else to say that they have a test that's going to tell me whether I got what *I* wanted out of it, well," she gives a small throaty laugh, "I don't consider that valid. Also, if you've come to a point where you feel in command of your own life, you don't need a test. I feel that a test is on a need basis, really. It's an ego basis. I didn't want that. If you need verification, then you're not really there. There are many philosophies where you reach a 'clear' point, but that's *your* 'clear' point. Nobody can test you on it. It's a personal concept. The clear that they mean is one that would make you available for Scientology. I saw that an attempt was being made not to let you have that state of clear. That they were going to use the notion, but were not going to allow it. And that's when I left."

Jerry has been listening, and now says: "I don't doubt that Hubbard—who I think is very impressive, a very good showman, very aware of many subjects, well-versed on many subjects—knows how to talk—working with a person could do great things. But when *he* does those great things and then writes a bulletin and says 'Everybody do this now with your preclears. . . .'" He gives a small shake of his head. "There are so many *human* situations going. Like all a guy can think about is screwing his auditor; many ego things going on. Like people being auditors, and that leading to a great deal of ego. There's a tremendous amount of unconscious activity going on down there and he just sends out a bulletin expecting the same results he gets. That's ludicrous. It's ludicrous for a person to think that he can start an *organization of teachers* like that and achieve the results he's achieving. In the Eastern sense, if he had brought one person to full enlightenment, it would have been much greater, than a thousand people to someplace lower." It is as if Hubbard no longer thinks of his followers as being plain old mortals. Says Jerry, "I remember a couple of guys who wanted to go into Reichian Therapy, and they talked about: 'Gee, it's great, you get these chicks in—you know, you work with people in the nude and you touch bodies. . . .' It's like here you can go in and become an auditor in very short order. A tremendous amount of pretense." He shakes his head again and then smiles. "I feel like James Coburn, in 'Flint,' when he goes up to the girl and says: 'You are not a something-something-Pleasure Machine.' That's how I feel with any scientologist: You are not a Hubbard Scientology computing machine."

II

Is Scientology brainwashing? Has L. Ron Hubbard actually developed a set of techniques which empty you of everything you are—your "self," however flawed—to be replaced with Scientology data: *theta*, Ability, MEST, Power, Past Lives, and all the rest of it? If, as Hubbard believed from the first moment he introduced Dianetics, the brain is a perfect computer, why can it not follow that he knows how to clean out that computer and reprogram it properly? You will probably argue that if Scientology is brainwashing, so is religious liturgy, and so is going to school, and so is . . . *anything* we learn. We think of brainwashing as being performed under duress, but Scientology involves genuine faith on the part of its participants. Can the label still apply?

The process of brainwashing, as defined in the *Encyclopaedia Britannica,* is "Controlling physical and social environment to destroy loyalties to any non-Communist—" the definition is given in terms of Chinese Communist methods "—groups or individuals, to demonstrate to the individual that his attitudes and patterns of thinking are incorrect and must be changed, and to develop loyalty and unquestioning obedience. . . . The process involves the removal of social and perceptual supports; the weakening of the ego by physical pressures; the coercion of guilt-provoking behavior that then requires rationalization; the destruction of the person's self-image by humiliation and revilement; the rebuilding of this self-image through the positive personal relationships that develop in the enforced intimacy of the cell despite the ever-present atmosphere of hostility; a shift of perceptual and semantic frames of reference resulting from the desire to identify with the point of view of the cellmates and the need to rationalize coerced behavior; and the elaboration of this new frame of reference through the intensive group study programs. The depth and permanence of these changes in attitude and point of view depend on the personality of the individual, his degree of motivation to be reformed and the degree to which the environment continues to coerce his behavior and support his new frame of reference."

Whatever physical and psychological cruelties this description implies as being inherent to successful brainwashing are missing, and, more important, unnecessary in Scientology for one simple reason: Scientologists *want* to be in Scientology because it works. It works because, quite simply, it is voluntary self-induced brainwashing. And because it does work, so many young people who have grown disillusioned with social structures which do not work at all, who refuse to accept the notion that life is an impossible struggle which cannot be made absolutely *simple*, find some kind of solace and welcome within a totally forgiving system which promises spiritual eternity, identifies and locates all guilt, and then—*mirabile dictu!*—makes it all go away, and replaces it with something glowing and sure. Scientology, whether you want to call it brainwashing or not, works because when all is said and done, the people in it do it to themselves.

Scientology's astonishing and continuing success is being additionally reinforced by a pervasive sense of togetherness which emanates from everything Scientologists do. I felt it at the Scientology Congress I attended at the Hotel Martinique and saw it in the steady stream of "successes" which pop up all over the place. It was never more evident than in the sense of beatific frenzy which welcomed the pre-Christmas appearance of John McMasters. All of these things work to give enormous strength to the belief that Scientology works.

What is even more impressive is the ease and speed with which people are smoothly made a part of the movement. Bud Lee, the young free-lance photographer who told me what happened during the first two sessions of the Communications Course, went into great detail about what it felt like when he first walked in. I think that both subjectively and objectively it gives a very revealing picture of what it is that helps make Scientology work.

"I went over on a Monday, and when I first came in, all I saw were all these happy people around—good-looking girls wearing these abbreviated costumes. One had on a little tiny brown miniskirt with a peekaboo see-through blouse, and she looked like something out of *Playboy*, but more earthy. There was this young guy on a couch, a very good-looking young guy, probably about twenty or twenty-one, and I don't know how many good-looking girls he had around: these girls were coming over, and they'd sit on his lap, and one girl, a big girl, a blonde, she came over and sat on his lap and started kissing him, and kissing his ears, and then she got up and left and a little while later *another* girl came over. I'd literally just come in off the street, I didn't know anything about Scientology at this point, other than a very small briefing [from someone at *Life* magazine]. It looked like one wild orgy. And the common expression, every time you say something, they say, 'Oh, *beautiful, beautiful.*' They're always saying, *'beautiful,'* with sort of a smile that's not a big smile, but sort of a benign smile. And these eyes that are not here nor there. They're like beautiful zombies, wandering around. So I was really enchanted by this whole atmosphere. Like I said, 'My God, if this is Hell . . . Wow! This is great! This is fantastic!' At *least* sixteen girls I saw that afternoon were really beautiful, really gorgeous! And I signed up for the $750 course, and I gave them a $50 down payment. And one girl came over to me and she sat down next to me and she said, real breathless, 'Hi, what's your name?' So I said, 'My name is Bud.' And she was really a gorgeous-looking girl, with long brunette hair, big hazel eyes, and very, very creamy white skin, and huge, soft breasts, and she just sat right next to me and began sorting out papers or something. And then she got up and said, 'Bye . . .' still breathy like that. 'I'll see you later.' "

From the first moments of confrontation in the Communications Course, Bud was taken by the whole thing. "At this point," he says, "I was still believing, I was sort of absorbing all this, and there were all these lonely people in the room: like there was a woman without a chin, and there was another girl who looked very kind of masculine, an uptight girl who had a leather outfit on. She was sweating. She didn't have any makeup. And there were all these kind of weird-looking people. And in addition to the weird-looking people there were some beautiful people, some really good-looking girls."

The next night, during the first break in Bull-Baiting, "this girl came in, Nina Jones, who looked like she just came out of *Glamour* magazine. She was wearing sort of a little Indian short minidress, and a band in her hair, and tight little curls, and necklaces, very cute looking, kind of peppy. And the moment she came into the room I *knew* she was in there for my benefit, because there was no other reason for her to be in that room. And she came over to me and said, 'Would you please come to my office? I'd like to talk to you.' She was very polite, you know, like they always are, with a sort of slight smile, and she said to me, 'Did you take any pictures?' And I said, 'Yes.' And I told her it was for a magazine. I don't remember all of it, but one question sticks in my mind, she kept repeating it over and over again—the same thing like we were having in Bull-Baiting: 'What were you doing on the third floor? What were you doing on the third floor? What were you doing on the third floor? What were you doing on the third floor?' Like that, over again and over again and over again. And doing it without showing anger, or anything, just over again and over again and over again. And I said, 'I wasn't *on* the third floor.' I said, 'Or if I *was* on the third floor, I didn't know I was on the third floor.' And then I suddenly remembered, and I said, 'Oh, yes, I remember yesterday, there was a monitor who took me up to get some tickets for a class on Saturday or something, and we went up to an upper level, and I thought it was the second floor,' and I said to her, 'Isn't this the first floor?' And she kind of looked at me, very suspiciously, with the same face though, and said, 'Who were you talking to on the third floor? Who were you talking to on the third floor? Who were you talking to on the third floor?' And I explained to her that I hadn't talked to anyone. Then I remembered that I had bumped into somebody I had met in Key West last January, a sculptor I had met down there. He was in this hallway and they had these rows of chairs and they were stuffing envelopes. They were all like these zombies with these slight smiles, sort of, you know, looking up. They were all stuffing envelopes, stuffing envelopes. And he got up and practically kissed me. He threw his arms around me, and he said, 'Oh, man! You're beautiful!' He's one of these really hip people, with big moustaches and the mod clothes . . . he's in his forties, but he acts like he's fifteen. He's the type of guy who says, 'How's your ass?' and all that sort of thing. And I said to him, 'When're you going to be leaving?' So we went out and had coffee. Anyway, that's the person I talked to. He's perfectly innocent, he didn't know I was coming. I didn't know he'd be there or anything. But Nina was convinced that I had been on the third floor and I had taken pictures of something on the third floor that I shouldn't have. I have no idea what's on the third floor other than the hall with the envelope stuffers. I know there's something in those rooms, but I didn't get to see the rooms, because there's a desk, with a girl behind it—same kind of smile—that separates you, and beyond her, who knows what goes on. If I was crazy, I'd suddenly imagine it's because they do it in the nude or something. But I really don't know what they do.

"So Nina examined me further, and then she mentioned Yvonne Chabrier, who is the reporter from *Life*, the researcher, she mentioned her name, and asked, 'Do you know Yvonne Chabrier? Do you know Yvonne Chabrier? . . . Yvonne Chabrier?' And I said, 'Yes, I do.' I didn't want to lie; I felt very *funny* lying. And she said, 'How do you know her?' and I said, 'Well, I originally came over here for *Life*, but they've already closed the story.' And then she *really* got uptight, and she walked out of the room, and said, 'I want you to come with me and meet this other guy,' I forget his name, Owen, or something, and he was in one of these little cubicles. And he sat down and he was much nicer. He did the same thing of cross-examining me, but he was more interested in what *Life* was doing. I explained to him that I didn't know what *Life* was up to, which I really didn't, because they had briefed me very little."

When it was all over, Bud not only apologized for what he had done, but turned over all of his film, exposed and unused. "I explained to them that I really *believe* in this stuff and that I thought they were doing a lot of good for a lot of people that had nothing else. That I would like to come back sometime, in the future, and take it up seriously. And they said, 'Maybe, in the future.' He, the guy, explained to me that I couldn't stay simply because I hadn't come of my own accord. They only are interested in people who come on their own; even if your *brother* sent you, he said, 'We won't take you. You come because *you* want to come.' So, Nina gave me my fifty-dollar deposit back, and I went back and got my coat in the room, and I thanked the teacher, Bobbie, and I spent too long talking to her, because Nina came in and she was very uptight about me talking to Bobbie, and Bobbie was confused. I said, 'Thank you very much, I hope to meet you again in the future.' And Nina kind of looked at her, and then looked at me, and I said to Bobbie, sort of, like, 'Nothing to worry about.' And then I put my coat on, and went home."

Bud pauses in his narrative and looks back on the whole experience, and then says, slowly, "I really did believe. I believed right until the moment they came and took me out of the class. I was like one of those lonely souls, I felt just like the other people in the class. . . ." He tries to laugh, but it goes dry. "There are really beautiful people in this, and I was really upset when they asked me to leave. I really was. I was more upset than they were. Because I wanted to find out, like I'm *dying* to find out what happens in the Fourth or Sixth Class. I wanted to see what they *did*. They really fed me the bait, and I bit!" He starts to laugh again, but instead stops and says, wistfully, "The girl who gave the first lecture, Bobbie, was beautiful. She sat on the edge of this desk, and crossed these long legs of hers, and these big eyes, and she was very soft-spoken, and she said, 'Now is there *anything* you don't understand?' "

A few weeks later, Bud received a letter from the Church of Scientology which began "Dear Bud," and expressed something akin to sorrow that he had asked for his money back. It went on to express the hope that he would return, that whatever had happened could be worked out and forgotten. When we last talked, Bud was seriously considering returning so that he could find out, finally, what does happen in the Fourth or Sixth Class.

Yes, Scientology may be a form of voluntary brainwashing, but conversely, we, as social animals, seem to *need* phenomena such as Scientology. Rollo May, the well-known psycho-therapist, discussed this question when he reviewed Dr. Winter's book, *A Doctor Looks At Dianetics,* in 1951. May suggested that there is something in us which is satisfied by a psycho-sociological movement which, as he put it, is a "confusion of fantasy with scientific claims. Apparently," he wrote, "modern people reach out on the one hand for scientific authority and on the other hand they seek some realm of fantasy in which their irrational tendencies can temporarily have full play." Speaking then as a behavioral scientist, May concludes: "Does this imply that modern man is not only anxious, demanding security, but also suffers in our commercial and industrial society from a suppression of fantasy life and imagination, and thus seizes upon the new forms of magic?" Nineteen years after that was written, with life accelerated to an almost maniac pitch, and a burgeoning interest in all forms of the occult as offering us some kind of an *answer,* man is looking to the seemingly irrational to explain the irrationality of modern times. The answer to May's question is Yes. If it were otherwise, Scientology would be unheard of and, though Hubbard would be the last to admit, unnecessary.

### III

Scientology inures itself against outside criticism by insisting that anything written or said against it must be judged relatively, viewed against the equally "relative" merits of other forms of psychotherapy and spiritual activity, and be seen in a "proper" context. When *Life* magazine published the long article on Scientology in 1968, L. Ron Hubbard wrote the magazine a letter in which he said: "Those attacking Scientology run mental institutions. They make millions out of it. They advocate brutal, murderous actions against the insane. They are terrified of losing the avalanches of money gouged out of governments. They see Scientology taking it all away with kind, effective measures. There is no question in their minds but that Scientology works. That's why they are attacking it. A thousand other philosophies and religions arise every year with no outcry from the madmen in charge. The hundreds of thousands of victims of the enemy, as in all fascist actions, cannot complain. They cannot even talk. They're dead."

Such an answer has become quite traditional with Hubbard. In an HCO Bulletin of May 5, 1959, he wrote: "The person who goes to a psychiatrist usually finds himself betrayed. He does not receive help, he receives brutality in the form of electric shocks, brain surgery and other degrading experiences. Even in the highest form of psychiatry it was common advice for the psychiatrist to tell the wife that the best cure for her troubles was to betray her husband, and vice versa." Surprisingly enough, when not speaking from what sounds interestingly close to personal experience, Hubbard has on occasion acknowledged that processing might cause a "nervous breakdown" which would require "observation" in a mental hospital. Describing what he named the "Sad Effect" in an HCO Policy Letter, he wrote: "We could call this Tearculi Apathia Magnus and everyone would be in great awe of it. But I see no reason to follow the Latinated nonsense of yesterday's failed sciences. Call it something simple and the auditor will feel he can do something about it and even the preclear will cheer up a bit. So it is 'the Sad Effect.' This is a state of great sadness, apathy, and misery and desire for suicide."

In Hubbard's now rare confrontations with the outside world, I found that you can never be sure whether he will be precise and decisive, as when he discusses the computer-like qualities of the mind and the statistical perfection of Scientology's *Standard Tech*, or mildly introspective and almost puzzled, as when, while discussing man's brain and its function during that filmed interview which is shown at all the free introductory Scientology sessions, he suddenly interrupts him-

self to say, "What it [the brain] does? Well, I'm not quite
sure. . . ." And some moments later, in this same film, discussing the insane, he says, "The insane are, well, they're
insane." This is not to imply that Hubbard is ever at a loss
for something to say. He measures the mood of a moment, and
then, with persistently winning charm, satisfies or confounds
a critic or questioner with just the right answer. The last question asked by the interviewer who accompanied the British
film crew which visited Hubbard on board his flagship
was "Do you ever think that you might be quite mad?"
I half expected Hubbard to rise up in righteous wrath and
indignation and summarily order the intruders off the vessel,
but he merely rolled the question over in his mind and then
said, with obvious relish, "Oh, yes! The one man in the world
who never believes he's mad, is a madman." And his broad
face, giving him the look of a homey, beardless Santa Claus,
split into a wide grin of sheer pleasure.

Recently, Eric Barnes, the Church of Scientology's public
relations director for the Eastern U.S., appeared as part of a
panel discussion on a television program and said, "Nowhere
in all the eighteen years of attacks that have been made against
Scientology—and always done in the same pattern—nowhere
has anyone come up with one person who has been harmed
by Scientology." What Barnes meant was that the cases on
record involving individuals who have taken Scientology
processing and ended up in mental hospitals cannot be introduced as evidence against Scientology because these persons
were unwell before Scientology ever touched them. When Dr.
Lewis L. Robbins, a prominent practicing psychiatrist who
was also on the program, asked Barnes if Scientology makes
an effort to determine whether or not someone might be emotionally or psychologically unfit, Barnes answered: "When
someone walks in who's obviously rational, who sits and
talks. . . . We discover that someone has had institutional
processing, or has been treated by a shock treatment, or

lobotomy, or leucotomy, which are the *tools* of the psychiatric trade, or convulsive drugs of one kind, we say, 'We're sorry, we cannot help you.' And that is the end of it." Simplistic but neat.

So the onus of any criticism is put on the critic. And what Hubbard knows is really sticking in everyone's craw is the fact that Scientology works! The only alternative for me then is to make some further observations about Hubbard's stubbornly heuristic approaches, and see where that leads.

Rollo May, in his review of Dr. Winter's book, wrote: "The one useful point in dianetics, in my judgment, is helping the patient to experience his feelings. Yet even this is not original: it is a form of abreaction, one of Freud's earliest techniques. As any psychologist knows, the difficulty is that the event about which the patient works out his feelings usually has no demonstrable relation to present reality. . . ."

This question of somehow defining what is fantasy and what is real brings us to some questions regarding the E-Meter, that indispensable Scientology tool which John McMasters, the world's first *clear*, has said measures "disagreements," not lies. In his already quoted study of the polygraph, or lie detector, Dr. Burke M. Smith stated: "To be effective an instrument or a test must be valid and it must be reliable." No attitude could be more scientific, pragmatic, and in accord with what Hubbard has said over and over again. Dr. Smith went on to explain that sufficient evidence to evaluate the polygraph was lacking because "in the few cases in which effectiveness has been evaluated, confessions of guilt or attempts to deceive have been commonly taken as criteria for determining validity. The trouble with this is that in many cases the confession may have come before or during the examination, which is thereupon said to have been conclusive!" Dr. Smith cites a specific example, the case of a young bank manager who was subjected to what Smith called a "routine" polygraph examination. "He showed violent response to the question: 'Have you ever stolen any money from the bank or its customers?' On a peak-of-tension test to specify the amount of money stolen, he showed strong reactions at the mention of the sums $800 and $1,100. He could not remember taking any such sum but, confused and convinced of the machine's infallibility, he confessed to having stolen $1,000 and told how he must have done it. The bank's auditors could find no such shortage or manipulation, and so the manager was referred for psychiatric examination." It was found that "the patient had strongly ambivalent feelings about his mother and wife and felt guilty about personal financial dealings with them involving the sums of $800 and $1,100. Both the mother and the wife were customers of the bank."

The same polygraph test was repeated by another examiner who also concluded that the bank manager was lying and must be guilty of theft because of his responses to questions where the word "customer" was used. Dr. Smith wrote: "Clearly the original polygraph results were not valid. It was not deception but an autonomic response to unconscious attitudes that had caused the strong polygraph reactions. The same effect was shown on a trivial question included as a control: 'Do you drink coffee?' The manager answered, quickly and truthfully, 'Yes,' but the polygraph showed a strong emotional reaction. The young man could not explain this, but psychotherapy revealed that coffee-drinking had been absolutely forbidden during his childhood; the memory of that prohibition had been lost or suppressed but remained potent. . . . In fact," Dr. Smith concluded, "any word that happens to have strong emotional connotations for an individual and that is included in a critical question may elicit a response that is erroneously attributed to an attempt at deception."

Dr. Smith describes other "pitfalls that can lead to 'false positive' or 'false negative' interpretations of a record. Some people are emotionally highly sensitive even to supposedly neutral stimuli; others are unresponsive. A person who believes what he says is true may show no emotional response even when he says what is objectively untrue. A person who is ashamed of his name may show emotion when he quite truthfully answers 'Yes' to 'Is your name Adolf Schicklgruber?'"

Finally, Dr. Smith raises certain ethical questions. "To say or imply," he wrote, "that the machine is infallible is to use a lie to detect a lie. To elicit admissions through fear of the machine or misrepresentation of its record is to force a confession. . . . A person undergoing even a routine polygraph test may inadvertently reveal, particularly in the preexamination interview, information about himself that he would not voluntarily have revealed. The polygraph operator is not a physician or a lawyer or a priest; he is anxious to pass on whatever details he can find to his superior or to the man who has hired him. If his findings cast doubt (rightly or wrongly) on the integrity or reliability of his subject or reveal idiosyncrasies or weaknesses, the subject's welfare or entire career may be harmed. Can such invasions of privacy be justified? It is said that taking a polygraph test is voluntary. Is it really voluntary, however, if a refusal can be interpreted as evidence of guilt or seems likely to jeopardize a job?"

Yet Scientology uses the E-Meter as an infallible tool in identifying and locating the most fundamental element of man: his spirit. And people being processed trust auditor and meter implicitly, not only because of Scientology's aura of religious counseling and benevolence, but because the needle *does* react, and the auditor seems to know *why*. One girl I talked to, who had taken assist auditing because she was having serious problems with her boyfriend, who was a Scientologist, said, of her auditor and the meter: "I never doubted that he was *capable* of auditing me. As I remember it, vaguely, he would ask me to take the cans in my hands, which of course at first horrified me—these jam cans in your hands—and the E-Meter would react. I always believed I made it react, if I had something on my mind."

The fact that a polygraph, much less an E-Meter, is incapable of telling fact from fiction is totally ignored by Scientology. People spin tales of past lives as Mark Antony, Cleopatra, being zapped by nasty Martians on some distant planet, pinpointing a dramatic moment 38 trillion years back, and come away from an auditing session convinced they have been telling the truth. It is as if Scientology ultimately *wants* everyone to believe in Gorilla Goals and "Boo-Hoos" and Being Three Feet In Back Of Your Head.

## IV

It is naïve and facile simply to label Scientology a fraud and a con; that is not even the point. A con is when you get somebody to pay out money for something you say you will do for them, or sell them, and then you do neither. Scientology gives its disciples *exactly* what it promises, from the very first moment a lecturer defines "reality" in Hubbard's terms. If, at that moment, you "agree," you accept the definition and believe yourself to be a bundle of chaotic distortions and spiritual contradictions which Hubbard's system *can* salvage and enshrine in the universe as a truly free-floating spirit, then Scientology obviously succeeds. The only question you have to ask yourself is whether or not L. Ron Hubbard's vision of life is one you fundamentally agree with. Everything else, the now-terminated "suppressions," the heartbreaking disconnections, the so-called "billion-year" contracts which bind youngsters to Scientology for "ever," the accusation that it is tampering with people's minds, all that is secondary. That may sound outrageous to you, but every step of Scientology evolves from the several declarations L. Ron Hubbard makes about what life *really* is. If you agree with his basic assumptions, then whatever tampering is done to your psyche is nothing less than what you have "agreed" you want done so that you, too, can achieve that perfect state of emptiness which he defines as clear.

It is a cruel truth, but one I feel I must subscribe to if I am to believe that any sincere determination to keep people from hurting themselves is not enough to justify banning a philosophy or religion. In a society which chooses to call itself free, any body of thought can call itself a philosophy and any one individual can found a religion.

If you can make yourself forget the menace of Scientology's Ethics, and forget about some of Hubbard's weirder inventions, one thing remains as a simple and genuine danger. Scientology's intention is to create a Brave New World with no room for outsiders, which, if you stop and think for a moment, is you and me. The pitiable converse to this already occurs every time a devoted scientologist leaves the warmth and security of any of Scientology's intensely active centers— remember that every Scientology office *always* has something going on—and returns, for a time, to the erratic panorama of contemporary society. I know of several instances when members of families have returned from Los Angeles, home of Scientology's American Saint Hill Organization, or from England, or particularly from the Sea Org, one of Hubbard's floating sanctums, and for two days have impressed their loved ones with the love and purity which seems to glow from their very being. Then, because they are not surrounded by fellow Scientologists whose presence recharges their cells with the Right Words and predetermined responses to that constant expression of Scientology's truths, these people dim and darken. Nothing around them seems sufficiently real. It is as if they have come down off a very sweet and shining trip, and only a return to the safety of their Scientology world will restore their functioning realities.

Finally, I don't really know what L. Ron Hubbard believes. I've often wondered whether or not he ever read Dr. Nordenholz's book with its dry postulatings of what might be done with man's consciousness, or whether Buckminster Fuller's vivid blasts about the Game of Life made more than a passing impression. When he wrote of his visit to Heaven in his HCO Bulletin of May 11, 1963, complete with a description of the Gates, was he only speaking in allegory? Does he really believe that *thetans* have done all the things he has written and said they have done, possess all the powers they are presumed to possess; and raising Scientologists to an advanced level of ability where they will be able to absorb it all is the true heart of Scientology? Or is it simply a brilliantly conceived system of programming a human being so that after a certain amount of "processing," at a certain level, he will be prepared to believe . . . *anything?*

When all of L. Ron Hubbard's theories and mouthings are reduced to their essentials, when the *thetan* stands alone, stripped of his theological trappings of "games," "past lives," "randomity," "time tracks," and "implants," one tiny, nagging suspicion lingers on: Is it possible that all of us are simply involved in yet another of this man's vivid flights of fantastic fiction, and it is all nothing less than a superbly evoked living nightmare, manipulated somewhere by a giant typewriter in the sky?

# EPILOGUE

On Friday, November 21, 1969, John McMaster, the first human on earth to achieve Scientology's beatific enlightenment known as Clear, sat down and wrote a long letter to his leader and mentor, L. Ron Hubbard. He began by recounting his unpleasant encounter in 1967 with the Sea Org's Ethics Mission—the Sea Org being Hubbard's floating arm, persistently expanding and making its presence felt by popping up just off shore from this or that Scientology organization to watchdog what was going on. McMaster recalled, gratefully, how Hubbard himself had stepped in to save him from the Ethics Mission; "You came to my rescue" is the way he expressed it. He went on to say that he had been wrong to let the matter drop at the time, "because what happened to me has happened in the last two years, unjustly to many, many people across the earth."

In his letter, McMaster described the activities of the Ethics Mission as "the tyranny [sic] of form monitoring function." Growing gently cautionary, he declared that "People are afraid to talk about their basic feelings even in a session. Many have told me so. Our organizations are not safe enough and hitting them with savage and vicious ethics does not help." The point he was making was that using Ethics to solve Scientology's problems was in reality creating greater and more dangerous problems. Then he dropped his bomb: he tendered his resignation from the Sea Org and thus from Scientology itself. His reason?

> So that such a thing of form monitoring function stops dead and it shall never happen to me or any other person again.

It is impossible to know from the letter whether one specific incident finally prompted the man to take a more careful look at what he had been living for so many years. He cites but two; the alleged kidnapping and dungeoning of an extremely successful Scientologist named Alan Walter, and the as-yet unsolved murders of two Scientologists in Los Angeles late in 1969. Concerning Walter, he wrote that the man "could not be the source of the current existing condition—" I assume a condition which would have been defined by Hubbard as representing a clear threat to Scientology. "Whatever his negative actions may or may not have been, they could have had no significance whatsoever if there had not been vast fields of fertile soil for them to grow in." What McMaster treats with such delicate circumspection is the wild rumor extant in Scientology circles that Walter had been called to a meeting with Hubbard when one of the ships was anchored off Cadiz. He had flown over, had been piped aboard with pomp and ceremony, and had then been seized, shackled, and thrown below decks where, the tale continues, he lingers even yet. Concerning the brutal killings of the two Scientologists, McMaster writes: "These last two ghastly murders of our students near ASHO in Los Angeles, one of whom is Clear, need never have happened, if we hadn't been mocking up Enemy so solidly." To interpret that as simply as possible, Scientology teaches its followers to deal with that which represents an Enemy by in effect giving it substance, a tangible reality—tiny clay figurines, for example—and then dealing with these mock-ups decisively. The only shattering conclusion to be drawn from what McMaster says is that these two had come to represent the Enemy so solidly for someone that they were dealt with too decisively. The casual possibility of this makes the blood run cold.

Hubbard's response to the McMaster letter—if one is to believe the lurid tale now circulating among those who fled the movement at about the same time—was to send some of his

Ethics squad over to Staten Island where McMaster was living and allegedly try to kidnap him. McMaster is said to have managed a telephone call to another formidable ex-Scientologist named Bernard Green, who in turn called McMaster's lawyer. The upshot of this story is that the Ethics mob melted away, apparently fearful of attracting the attention of local police. What followed sounds even more like a badly written espionage melodrama. Convinced that all airports were under surveillance by members of the Ethics Mission eager to grab him, McMaster was spirited on board a Greek freighter bound for his home, South Africa. Now safely there—he was met by his father who had apparently been alerted to local efforts at nabbing his son—he still entertains hopes of some kind of a rapprochement. At least that is what Bernard Green told me. He used that word, *rapprochement*, when he said a meeting had actually been proposed between McMaster, himself, and Hubbard on neutral territory, in Switzerland. Green seemed to find this perfectly plausible, that the three of them might all sit down and calmly discuss their various grievances. (Let me remind you again that an overwhelming number of former Scientologists would return to the movement instantly if they felt Hubbard had made certain sincere changes in the organization's structure.) McMaster himself closed his letter by saying he wished to return home and do "the Hubbard Standard Dianetic Course and continue to distribute our Tech to the people of earth." Obviously, he wanted to keep the door open, hoping still that Hubbard might see the tragedy of his ways and make some changes.

I suppose I can understand a man of the devotion of John McMaster closing his eyes to instances of inelegant punishment performed in the name of Scientology. After all, his own radiating sense of forgiveness, his electric innocence and apparent inner peace, have served as living proof that Scientology can indeed do what it claims. What I cannot understand is an offensive air of righteousness that pervades the conversations of some of the many other Scientologists who left simultaneously with the dissemination of the McMaster letter. Bernard Green, for example, who is a small, chunkily built man with an incessant bouncing joviality about him, claims to have been Hubbard's confidant for twenty years, from the very beginning, having assumed numerous responsibilities in spreading The Word to the four corners of the globe. He recounted some of the more grisly tales floating around throughout the movement's disenchanted members with a relish bordering on glee. The stories, none substantiated, are certainly terrifying: a seventy-two-year-old woman hurled down a flight of stairs by members of the Sea Org's Ethics Mission; two children, one five years old, the other four-and-a-half, put into chains on one of the Sea Org's ships; a man in Los Angeles punished for some anti-Scientological action by having high-pressure water hoses turned on him until he was pounded senseless. There is also an allegation that the Church of Scientology in Manhattan operates a "jail" in Brooklyn for enemies of the movement. The atrocities, and they can certainly be called that if true, seem to represent an inspiring aspect to be recalled by all who have left what one ex-Scientologist soberly refers to as "the paramilitary structure of Scientology."

Green, a man who clearly seems to be enjoying the upheaval he is part of, asked if I believed any of the stories. I could only say that they didn't sound impossible, considering that the policies of Scientology's Ethics do indeed exist, are available in one of the movement's widely sold books, and are apparently being energetically practiced by Hubbard's Sea Org Missionaries. What of course I cannot and will not understand, ever, is what took everybody so long if, as is now claimed, these horror stories have been common knowledge for literally years. Green's answer that all of them were being led on by what he calls "the golden carrot"—Hubbard's promise of Total Freedom—is totally inadequate. Unless, of course, they were led to believe not that Scientology was capable of developing and exploiting their existing abilities, but that it could and would make them all Super-Beings. Super-Beings, as history has taught us, can blithely ignore most of what goes on around them because they are involved in the business of being Super.

We must never forget that no matter what Hubbard has done, he has commanded an incredible affectionate loyalty from those who considered themselves close to him. Even today, with the news that Scientology has been fiscally re-organized from top to bottom so that 90 per cent and not 10 per cent of all monies will be paid in to Hubbard personally, even with Hubbard himself off on a new tangent, rhetorically asking his followers "Who is the Messiah?" only to answer with a parable involving a powerful, barrel-chested man with red hair, even now, John McMaster closes his letter as follows:

> I shall never withdraw my allegiance from your love or the product of your love, nor shall I withdraw allegiance from all people of earth and their attempts to attain Infinite Freedom, particularly those who work with our Tech to further man's attempts to attain Infinite Freedom.
> I shall continue to give your love to the world. As always, my love to you, (signed) John McMaster.

The entire letter, its tone so sincerely beseeching, so devoted, and—yes—so almost obedient, made me remember all over again the first time I had ever seen John McMaster. His manner in front of that adoring crowd, and his certainty, and his loving benevolence, and his infinite patience with that in all of us which is most uncertain—our capacity to *believe*—it all came back. And now he had quit. Once more, I heard him saying to all of us, "How can there be two sides to the truth?"

I think John McMaster may finally have answered that question for himself.